To the people of Mission San Juan Capistrano

MISSION
SAN JUAN CAPISTRANO
A PLACE OF PEACE

TEXT BY KATHLEEN WALKER   PHOTOGRAPHS BY MARC MUENCH

AZURITE™ BOOKS

ACKNOWLEDGMENTS

The author and editors extend special acknowledgment to individuals and organizations whose cooperation and assistance were invaluable in producing this book. They include: Gerald Miller, administrator, Mission San Juan Capistrano, and members of his staff; Reverend William Krekelberg, archivist at Mission San Juan Capistrano; Harry Francisco, archaeologist at Mission San Juan Capistrano; and the San Juan Capistrano Historical Society.

Book Designer: BARBARA GLYNN DENNEY
Photography Editor: PETER ENSENBERGER
Copy Editor: PK PERKIN McMAHON
Book Editor: BOB ALBANO
Decorative elements including keystones and map
of missions by Kevin Kibsey.
Additional photography by Peter Ensenberger.
Historical photo enhancement by Billie Jo Bishop.

Library of Congress Control Number 2002100707
ISBN 1-893860-65-5

First printing, 2002. Printed in Hong Kong.

Publisher: WIN HOLDEN
Managing Editor: BOB ALBANO
Associate Editor: EVELYN HOWELL
Associate Editor: PK PERKIN McMAHON
Art Director: MARY WINKELMAN VELGOS
Director of Photography: PETER ENSENBERGER
Production Director: CINDY MACKEY

Front and back covers:
Aged but solid, arches frame the Entry Courtyard at Mission San Juan Capistrano, and flowers, plants, and trees add a sense of elegance. A huge pepper tree, dating to the late 1800s, is at left. Here, a visitor faces north, looking toward a wing that once housed a vestment room and living quarters. Today's gift shop (once a chapel) is in the wing behind the arches at right.

Dedication and Page 96:
A Kevin Kibsey painting shows the original keystone in the center dome of the Great Stone Church. A keystone locks pieces of an arch together. Mission builders expressed great pride in their work by imbuing keystones, even those that generally would not be seen by the public, with decorative touches.

Page 2:
Draped by bougainvillea, an arch that's part of the original Mission San Juan Capistrano remains suspended in time and beauty at the end of the South Wing. This arch also is shown in a historical photo for the year 1829 in the timeline on Pages 10-11.

Pages 6-7:
The Central Courtyard, laced with lawns, flower gardens, paths, and the mission's main fountain (right side) lies between the South Wing (foreground) and North Wing (middle). The end of the series of arches in the foreground also is shown on Page 2. Domes of the Basilica of San Juan Capistrano are seen through the arch at left. The bell tower is atop the North Wing.

CONTENTS

Fitting for a contents page, these thumbnail photos show major elements of Mission San Juan Capistrano. In the center image, graceful lilies grow alongside the rough textures of an arch and plastered wall of the Serra Chapel. The images at left and right show views from the Entry Courtyard, including portions of the Bell Wall and ruins of the Great Stone Church.

PROLOGUE

PATHWAYS

The images flow like a river of silk. A child's hand reaches out from the pews of the tiny chapel and pats gently on the adobe wall. The touch seems one of recognition and reassurance. Outside, a far older hand pats a paving stone on a meandering path. The man, like many others, has dedicated a stone in memory of a loved one.

In one courtyard, a group of school children surrounds a silver-haired woman. She wears the red, black, and white colors that mark her as their mission guide. "Oh," she says, the pleasure in her face matching the joy in theirs, "you are the smartest group." Then they move on in a close-knit circle of excitement.

They all have come to spend an hour or a day or a lifetime at Mission San Juan Capistrano, 64 miles north of San Diego, California. Born in the time of an empire, the mission has drawn the faithful and the curious for more than 200 years.

The mission presents its beauty like its secrets, slowly. Outside the walls, you get only a hint, a coral-colored rose reaching just above one wall, pastel budded hollyhocks rising above another. Once inside, you move from garden to garden, from archway to arcade, drawn always deeper into the compound and into history.

Paths meander through flower beds and rosebushes and radiate from around a fountain like spokes of a wheel lying on an emerald green lawn. Some paths hug buildings, moving from room to room, from century to century. One room holds the simple austerity of a priest pledged to poverty. Another room offers up the frills of the gentility of family life in the 1860s. Many of the paths lead to and around the ruins of a church that rose more than five stories before falling first to the power of nature and then to the well-meaning actions of men.

Sit in one small garden and you see both a wall of bells and a wall of boulders. One man could ring those bells, but a village of men had to move those rocks, had to raise them high, believing that what they built would stand long beyond themselves.

Sit in the gardens of the Central Courtyard and you see hills of California's Coastal Range beyond the mission. No houses cling to the tops, no developments block the view. The town beyond the walls gave the mission this gift, protecting the hilltops by law so that the vision of the past would remain unchanged. The loveliness of this place has many dimensions and many protectors.

They wrote a song about this mission and the swallows that made their own pilgrimages here. Some people made movies at the mission. Some searched for treasure. Others looked for a home. In the early 1900s, a traveler of many roads stopped by the mission and helped build a garden. Then he went back to the road, only to be robbed. He wrote to the priest that he wished to take his own path back to the mission, where he had known kindness.

"Yes, John," replied the priest, "you are welcome to come and stay a while . . ."

One mission path leads to the chapel, tiny and quiet. Sit here and you hear nothing of the modern world, no town life, no visitors' voices, no pulsating movement of traffic on a freeway full of people going somewhere fast. You do hear the songs of the birds in the gardens outside, rising like the glow of the candles within the chapel. In this place of peace, where Mission San Juan Capistrano really began, you also may wish to reach out and gently pat the wall.

MISSION TIMELINE

1683 Jesuits begin developing line of missions on Baja California Peninsula.

1713 Nov. 24, Father Junípero Serra is born and baptized Miguel José in Petra on the Spanish island of Majorca.

1732 Benjamin Franklin publishes *Poor Richard's Almanac.*

1767 Spain expels Jesuits from empire. Franciscans take over missions in Baja California.

1700 250,000 settlers live in North American colonies.

1730 Fr. Serra joins the Order of Friars Minor, the Franciscans.

1749-1750 Fr. Serra arrives in Mexico.

Fr. Serra begins missionary work in Sierra Gorda region of central Mexico.

1768 Fr. Serra begins assignment as president of the missions of Baja California.

1806 Great Stone Church dedicated.

1821 Mexico wins independence from Spain.

1829 Author Alfred Robinson describes Mission San Juan Capistrano as "lonely, dilapidated."

1841 Town of San Juan Capistrano is founded.

1812 Dec. 8, earthquake destroys Great Stone Church, killing 40 people at morning mass.

1823 July 4, last of 21 missions is founded, San Francisco Solano, north of San Francisco.

1835 Richard Dana, author of *Two Years Before the Mast,* begins his travels on California coast.

1843 First wagon train of settlers from U.S. arrives in California.

1869 Suez Canal opens.

Work begins on the Brooklyn Bridge.

1891 Sir Arthur Conan Doyle's *The Adventures of Sherlock Holmes* is published.

1896 Landmarks Club begins reroofing, rebuilding mission walls, stabilizing Great Stone Church.

1910 Mexican Revolution begins.

Fr. St. John O'Sullivan arrives, continues restoration of Mission San Juan Capistrano and invites artists to paint at the mission.

1887 California Railroad arrives in town of San Juan Capistrano, spurring tourism.

1895 Charles Lummis founds Landmarks Club to preserve historic landmarks of California.

1905 Einstein presents his Theory of Relativity.

1914 World War I begins.

1769 July 16, Fr. Serra founds Mission San Diego de Alcalá, the first of 21 California missions to be established in a line running north for 650 miles.

1775 Oct. 30, Fr. Fermín Lasuén founds Mission San Juan Capistrano, then abandons it due to uprising at San Diego.

1775–1783 American Revolution.

1777 Jan. 23, first marriage at the mission, Saturnino and Brigida.

July 13, first burial, the girl Sinforosa.

1789 French Revolution begins with the storming of the Bastille.

1772 Records show five missions have been founded, 491 baptisms performed.

1776 Nov. 1, Fr. Serra formally founds Mission San Juan Capistrano.

Dec. 19, first baptism, the boy Nanagibar, baptized as Juan Bautista.

July 4, Declaration of Independence.

1784 Aug. 28, Fr. Serra dies at Mission San Carlos Borromeo, 70 years old.

1797 First stones are laid for massive stone church; building continues for nine years.

1845 Mission San Juan Capistrano sells at auction for $710, becomes private residence of the Forster family.

1848 January, gold is discovered at Sutter's Mill.

Feb. 2, Mexico cedes California to the U.S. under the Treaty of Guadalupe Hidalgo.

1850 Sept. 9, California becomes a state.

1861–1865 American Civil War.

1846 United States declares war on Mexico.

1849 California Gold Rush, tens of thousands arrive by sea and land.

Reinforced concrete is introduced in France.

1860s All but two remaining domes of Great Stone Church are blown up by townspeople who believe them to be unsafe.

1865 March 18, President Abraham Lincoln signs document restoring mission to the Catholic Church.

April 15, President Abraham Lincoln is assassinated.

1922–1924 Gold altar and altar pieces are installed in Serra's Chapel.

1939 World War II begins with German invasion of Poland.

Leon Rene writes the song, *When the Swallows Come Back to Capistrano*.

1988 Fr. Serra is beatified by Pope John Paul II, second of three steps to declaration of sainthood.

2002 Mission San Juan Capistrano continues to attract hundreds of thousands of visitors from around the world.

1929 U.S. Stock Exchange collapses; Great Depression begins.

1950 World population reaches 2.3 billion.

1989 Major project begins to restore, stabilize, and preserve buildings of mission compound.

San Francisco de Solano †

San Rafael Arcángel †

SAN FRANCISCO

San Francisco de Asís †

San José de Guadalupe †

Santa Clara de Asís †

Santa Cruz †

San Juan Bautista †

San Carlos Borromeo de Carmelo †

Nuestra Señora de la Soledad †

San Antonio de Padua †

San Miguel Arcángel †

San Luis Obispo de Tolosa †

la Purísima Concepción †

Santa Inés †

Santa Bárbara †

San Fernando Rey de España †

San Buenaventura †

San Gabriel Arcángel †

LOS ANGELES

San Juan Capistrano †

San Luis Rey de Francia †

San Diego de Alcalá †

SAN DIEGO

PACIFIC OCEAN

ALTA CALIFORNIA

San Juan Capistrano

EL CAMINO REAL

A ROYAL LINE

KINGS AND QUEENS

One ruled as "The Queen," Santa Barbara; another as "The King," San Luis Rey de Francia; and San Diego de Alcalá wore the crown as the first of the line. They were part of the chain of 21 missions that ran the length of Spanish California from San Diego to Sonoma. They marked stops on *El Camino Real,* "The Royal Road." Four *presidios,* or forts, also stood watch along the California coast, at San Diego, Santa Barbara, Monterey, and San Francisco.

For 60 years, a few hundred soldiers and a handful of priests in gray robes served these structures of empire in the absolutely impossible task of holding back the onslaught of revolution, liberation, greed, and growth.

This Catholic mission chain came late to the New World holdings of Spain. Missions had been established in the early 1600s in what now is New Mexico. Another mission system, running from the northern Mexican state of Sonora to what now is Arizona, was founded in the late 1680s by Father Eusebio Kino, the Jesuit priest and explorer. Mission building in Texas began during the same period.

Spain had long and deep claims to the territory at the northern edge of its empire. In 1535, 16 years after he began his march on the Aztecs, Hernán Cortés placed his boots and his ambitions on the rocky land of *Baja* (lower) *California.* Mexico had given him gold and silver. This time he searched for pearls. In 1539, Friar Marcos de Niza walked from Mexico into Arizona and New Mexico in search of the fabled cities of Cíbola with Esteban, the Moor, guiding the way. Coronado marched for those same cities of gold in 1540, getting as far as the present state of Kansas.

But, seaborne treasure did not prove enough for Cortés. He left *Baja* after two years. De Niza never located the fabled cities, and Esteban found only death in the New Mexico land of the Zuni. Coronado may have seen Kansas, but he never saw any golden towers.

The Spanish also had claims on the vast piece of land above *Baja.* The explorer Juan Rodríguez Cabrillo had sailed into the bay at San Diego in 1542. The explorer Sebastian Vizcaino had sailed the northern coast of California in 1602 and noted the bay that would be called Monterey. The Pacific Ocean fell to the Spanish, earning it the nickname "The Spanish Lake" due to the caravans of galleons

Twenty-one missions form a chain along *El Camino Real,* "The Royal Road," on the map of Spanish California, opposite page. The Spaniards called this region *Alta,* or upper, *California.* Lower California is *Baja California.*

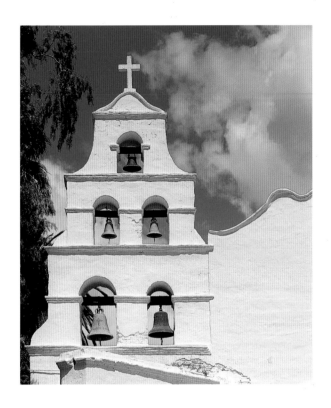

The first in the mission chain, San Diego de Alcalá, opposite page, continues to serve both as an active parish and a major tourist destination. In 1775, the native population attacked, burning the mission and killing a priest. The uprising delayed establishment of Mission San Juan Capistrano to the north.

The 46-foot-tall bell wall of Mission San Diego de Alcalá was reconstructed in the 1930s.

carrying the treasure trade of Asia back to the empire.

The English had their own claim to California. Francis Drake, explorer and patriot to the English, pirate and worse to the Spanish, landed north of San Francisco in 1579 while searching for a northwest passage between the Pacific and north Atlantic oceans. He claimed the land for his queen, Elizabeth I, daughter of Henry VIII, the king who ended the supremacy of the Catholic Church in his realm. Good Queen Bess to her people, she was heretic and foe to the Spanish.

Still, in the annals of conquest, the Spanish got to California first. What the rulers of Spain lacked, and would for the next two centuries, was the incentive to go back and take possession.

The land above *Baja* offered a temptation, a native people who could be brought to Catholicism. Contemporary estimates of California's native population at the time of the first European explorations run at about 300,000, although some go as high as 500,000. But souls for the church and *Baja* pearls could not compare to the treasure troves of the Aztecs and Incas. Conquistadors had found gold enough in those empires to fill a thousand galleons. They had found mountains filled to the netherworld with silver. The Spanish saw their profits under the ground, not on it. The claim of one queen on a piece of territory that offered little could easily be ignored. Then, came an empress.

At a diplomatic party in St. Petersburg in 1768, Catherine the Great announced Russia's presence and interest in the northern coast of North America. Russian fur trappers had moved south from Russian holdings in Alaska, tempted by the fur-rich land of northern California. Her words sent a cloud of worry back to Madrid.

Carlos III of Spain acted quickly. He had the incentive. He had the claims. And, he had the Franciscans, the religious order that followed the teachings of St. Francis of Assisi. One of that brotherhood would be instrumental in building him an adobe and wood-beamed line of possession.

FATHER JUNIPERO SERRA

"Don't be so hard on Serra," Buena Ventura Albertina Garcia Nieblas used to tell her grandson Jerry Nieblas, who now works at the mission. He grew up, as she had, in the town of San Juan Capistrano. The family line goes back to the very beginning, to the time of Father Junípero Serra and the

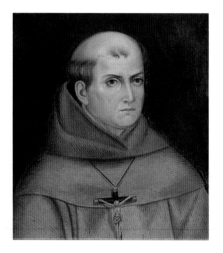

Reconstructed with assistance from a grant from the William Randolph Hearst Foundation, Mission San Antonio de Padua retains a sense of mission-era isolation. Father Junípero Serra founded the mission, his third, in 1771. The mission claims the honor of being the site of the first marriage in the mission chain, that of Juan Ruiz of Sonora, Mexico, and Margarita, a woman of the mission.

An original oil painting of Father Serra hangs at Mission Santa Barbara. An inscription below the portrait refers to him as Apostle of *Alta California*. Throughout his life in Mexico and California he suffered from a painful open wound on his leg, possibly caused by a spider or mosquito bite. The injury was said to have been treated once with ointment used for mules.

soldiers, and even farther back, to a time before the priests. Within the veins of this family runs the blood of the Acjachemen, the first people of this land. The Spanish gave them another name, Juaneño.

Everything about their world changed with the arrival of Serra and the Spanish on the coast of upper California. From that day in July 1769, when he founded the first mission at what is now San Diego, Serra would never again be far from greatness or controversy.

Born Miguel José Serra on the Spanish island of Majorca in 1713, he joined the Order of the Friars Minor, the Franciscans, while still a teenager. He took the name of Junípero, one of the companions of St. Francis of Assisi. He became a teacher at the Franciscan college in Palma, Majorca, counting among his students Father Francisco Palóu. Palóu would later become Serra's biographer and fellow missionary in California. He would be the one to record Serra's last days in the Book of the Dead at Mission San Carlos Borromeo in Carmel.

In 1749, Serra and Palóu did what thousands had done before them, pledged themselves to the missionary work of the New World. They would take the beliefs and the rituals of the Catholic Church to the unconverted of Mexico.

They would go, as had the others before them, with little hope of ever seeing their families again.

"I wish I could give them some of the happiness that is mine," Serra wrote of his family before leaving Spain, "and I feel that they would urge me to go ahead and never to turn back." He also wrote of his duty, "to do the Will of God."

That will took him to missionary work in the Sierra Gorda region of central Mexico and then to the capital, Mexico City, and the Franciscan College of San Fernando. At age 54, he received his assignment as president of the missions of *Baja California*. The Jesuits who had built them, the men of the black robes, had been ordered into exile.

Missionaries, explorers, scholars, the Jesuits had earned the animosity of Europe's royalty. They had a stiff-necked tendency to answer to a power beyond that of kings and to judge the often less-than-regal actions of their earthly lieges. Carlos III ordered them out of his empire, but the missions they left behind had to be manned.

The mission systems of the Spanish empire did not act solely as gathering centers for religious education and conversion. By design, they became agricultural enterprises, feeding soldiers and settlers and helping in the establishment of more missions. Now, with both Russia and Father

Serra in place, Carlos III called for a new chain.

Four expeditionary parties left *Baja California* for *Alta* (upper) *California* in the first months of 1769, two by sea and two by land. The parties included neophytes (Christianized Indians) from the *Baja* missions; soldiers; priests; the governor of *Baja California*, Don Gaspár de Portolá; and Father Junípero Serra.

Serra left with the last party for the five-week march north. He described the trip as a "truly happy one," in a wondrous land, a land rich with wild roses, ripe with wild grapes. He wrote of mountains, "Yes, plenty of them — and big ones too — but of pure soil," and wildlife. "We saw jackrabbits, cotton-tail rabbits and now and then a deer and a great number of antelope."

He wrote of the native people he met where the first mission would be built, San Diego. "They treat us with confidence and good will, as if they had known us all their lives." He did note that the initially friendly native people refused the food the Spanish offered them. They had good reason.

Scurvy had decimated the crew of one ship, the *San Carlos*. Two survived out of 26. The other ship, the *San Antonio*, left the sick and dying at San Diego and sailed south for more men and supplies. Portolá took a land

Mission San Gabriel Arcángel was so prosperous that one Spanish governor of California reported that it "has sustained the conquest of *Alta California*." Founded in 1771, the mission later hosted the expedition of more than 200 settlers and soldiers led by Juan Bautista de Anza, the founding citizens of San Francisco. Now rebuilt, the mission suffered earthquake damage in 1804, 1812, and 1987.

This manual for Franciscan missionaries, dedicated and signed by Father Serra, was brought by the priest from Mexico to California. He gave the book to his seventh mission, San Juan Capistrano, where it is kept in the archives.

expedition to the north to search for the great bay described by Vizcaino. They found the bay, Monterey, but not sufficient food for the return march. That they accomplished by eating their mules. In their absence, Serra officially founded Mission San Diego de Alcalá.

Portolá and his men made it back to camp to join the long wait for the *San Antonio*. The governor finally decided that if the ship had not returned by March 19, 1770, the dream of a mission chain would end with a retreat to the south. Serra requested a novena, nine days of prayer.

The original Mission San Diego no longer sits atop the hill near the sea. Five years after the founding, the priests moved the mission 6 miles inland. Nothing remains of the presidio that stayed and served on the site for 60 years. But, a statue of Serra still lingers in a shady garden. A man could pace in this garden, could walk out from under the trees, to scan the horizon a hundred times, waiting for a ship and the future to appear.

Both did arrive, on the ninth day of prayer, March 19, 1770, the feast of San José, St. Joseph's day. However, the *San Antonio* didn't stop but kept heading north to that bay of Vizcaino's. No matter, the deadline with fate had been met. The mission chain would be built. Four days later,

the *San Antonio* made an anticlimactic return to San Diego, having lost an anchor.

Serra sailed on the ship's next trip up the coast. At Monterey Bay, he founded the second mission and his headquarters, San Carlos Borromeo. The news of the two California missions sent the bells of Mexico City into a daylong frenzy of chimes. The king's claim to California had been cemented, as had the Church's claim to souls therein. For the next 14 years, Serra would oversee the interests of crown and church and create a written record of the work of the missions as well as of his own actions. The empire demanded paperwork.

IN HIS WORDS

Serra's letters and reports present a view of a man forced to deal with the minutiae of bureaucracy, while answering the basic needs of the missions, the spiritual needs of thousands of new arrivals to the religion, the requests of priests, actions of solders, demands of civil authorities, and the diplomatic niceties expected by representatives of the Crown. On some issues, polite palaver did not apply.

Mission San Carlos Borromeo in Carmel was founded in 1770. The present church was built in 1793 of sandstone and is noted for its bell tower of Moorish design, opposite page, and the star window over the front entrance, above.

The second in the chain, San Carlos Borromeo was the headquarters, home, and final resting place of Father Serra. Father Fermín Lasuén, the second great mission founder, who established nine missions after Father Serra's death, also is buried here near the main altar.

At Mission San Carlos Borromeo, a life-sized study in bronze shows Father Serra in death with the cowl of his robe raised over his head and his hands clasped in prayer. Father Juan Crespi stands in prayer at his fellow Franciscan's head. The memorial, created by artist Jo Mora, also depicts other priests and a grizzly bear cub, symbol of a young California. Seen through the doorway is the main altar. Father Crespi traveled with one of the two land expeditions from *Baja California* in 1769 and with the Portolá expedition, noting other possible mission sites, including that of San Juan Capistrano.

"The soldiers, without any restraint or shame have behaved like brutes towards the Indian women," he wrote to his superior in Mexico of conditions at one mission.

He had trouble with the soldiers and the *alcaldes*, the native overseers. He saw both abuse their power. He had trouble with the governors of California, and they had trouble with him. He once traveled back to Mexico City, more than 400 miles of the trip on foot, to complain in person about one governor, only to have him replaced by another not of his choosing.

The man who did get the office, Fernando Rivera y Moncada, wrote of his own frustrations with Serra: "He thinks of nothing but founding missions, no matter how or at what expense they are established." He did not mean the description as a compliment.

Serra founded five missions by 1772, three others by 1777. In 1779, Mission San Diego lacked food, floods hit Santa Clara, and Serra had problems with a governor. In 1780, he worried over the actions of some *alcaldes*. In 1782, he founded his ninth mission, San Buenaventura. He reported it all with an eye for the small events that make history interesting.

He wrote of what the native people on the beaches

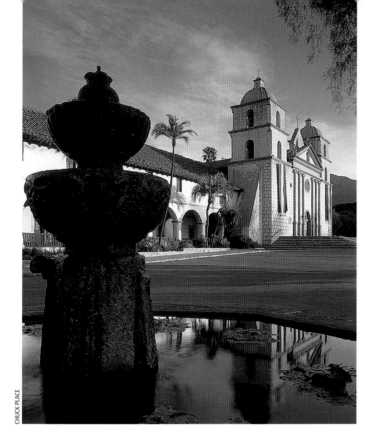

CHUCK PLACE

of San Diego did want instead of food. "From me they wanted my habit; from the governor his leather jacket, his waistcoat, breeches: in short, everything he wore."

He chronicled the events of his time that became the history of California and the United States. In 1775, Juan Bautista de Anza led a group of 240 settlers and soldiers from the Spanish presidio in Tubac, Arizona, to California. They would be the founding settlers of San Francisco. Anza had made an earlier trip to scout the route across the desert. On both visits, he was greeted at the missions of California as a favored guest.

Serra wrote they rang the bells for Anza, killed cows for him and chickens, baked him cakes, and gave him the ultimate mission treat, chocolate. Apparently, Anza did not return the hospitality.

Wrote Serra: "As to what he has given us in the way of mules, mares, cows, etc, not a single head did we get, nor has he ever said a word that would indicate that he ever, at any time, had any intention of bringing us any of them or anything else."

The staccato beat of angry words put to paper, the tight grip on the pen can still be sensed. But, that same hand would have a lighter touch when writing about the people he

met on the beaches and among the hills of California.

In 1775, a revolt by the native people against the mission of San Diego resulted in the death of a priest. Father Serra wrote to the viceroy of Mexico of his feelings toward the kind of punishment to be extracted.

". . . if ever the Indians, whether they be gentile or Christian, killed me, they should be forgiven," he wrote. "And as to the murderer, let him live, in order that he should be saved . . ."

Father Junípero Serra died on August 28, 1784, at age 70. He had worn the habit and the rope belt of the Franciscan order for more than 50 years. Father Palóu attributed his death to a chest ailment. His remains rest under the floor near the main altar of the church at Mission San Carlos Borromeo.

In 1988, the Catholic Church beatified Serra, the second of three steps to formal declaration of sainthood. Under his leadership thousands had been baptized, nine missions founded. Today only one church remains where Father Junípero Serra stood before the people he had come to save, a small adobe church at the mission they would call "The Jewel."

Two identical bell towers distinguish Mission Santa Barbara, "The Queen," above left, from other missions in the California chain. An active house of worship surrounded by manicured gardens, the church was built by local Chumash people to replace an earlier structure damaged by the earthquake of 1812.

Titled *La Christianita*, this 1776 sketch depicts Franciscan missionaries baptizing an infant of the Acjachemen, the native people of the area near San Juan Capistrano. The Spaniards called them Juaneño. The sketch is kept at the mission.

THE JEWEL

SETTING

The complex of Mission San Juan Capistrano covers 10 acres owned by the Catholic Diocese of Orange County, California. Built to house and educate a native population and to provide the goods for the survival of that population, the mission now hosts 500,000 visitors a year. This symbol of empire has become one of the major tourist attractions in southern California.

For the travelers of early California, the mission's location presented a welcome stopping point between Mission San Luis Rey, a day's ride south, and Mission San Gabriel, a day's ride north. For today's traveler, the location seems equally ideal, approximately halfway between the metropolitan areas of San Diego and Los Angeles, yet still in a small-town setting. Green hills roll to the east, the ocean to the southwest, and a Mediterranean climate softens both the air and the weather.

The Franciscans had their requirements for the location of a mission. They needed access to fresh water, arable land for livestock and crops, and a native population. The Portolá expedition found just such a site in 1769 in the valley of Santa Maria Magdalena near the Santa Ana

Arches and arcades at the edges of buildings, left, are inherent in the distinctive style of California missions such as Mission San Juan Capistrano. These arches are at the edge of an arcade flanking a wall of the Serra Chapel. Just beyond the arches lies the Central Courtyard, above, laced with lawns, flowers, and paved pathways. In the mission era, the courtyard was a hub of activity, giving it a utilitarian look.

Mountains and San Juan Creek.

The surrounding land presented a rich tapestry of vegetation, grassland, brush, sycamores, and oaks. According to one historic account, the friendly natives of the area offered the Spanish expedition gifts of "their poor seeds." If they were acorns, the Spanish had been given a generous gift. Acorns provided a staple in the diet of the Acjachemen.

Contemporary scholars believe this to be the area where Mission San Juan Capistrano was first established. Within three years, a need for a more dependable water supply resulted in a move a few miles to the southwest where the mission now stands.

The name for the mission had already been chosen, next on the list of names sent north by the viceroy. San Juan Capistrano, the patron saint of Hungary, would be honored. This Franciscan priest had served as a representative of the pope in 15TH century central Europe. In 1456, at age 71, he led a wing of a Christian army against the Turkish invaders of Hungary. The battle won, he then died of a fever.

The founding of the mission christened in his name took place on October 30, 1775, with the necessary religious steps of a blessing of the site and a Mass. And while Father Serra is almost always mentioned in connection with the birth of this mission, he did not officiate. He sent Father Fermín Francisco de Lasuén from Mission San Diego. Lasuén would go on to be the other great mission builder of California, founding nine missions after Serra's death.

"We had erected the mission cross, enclosed a spacious corral, mapped out the building, dug the holes in which to insert the poles," Lasuén wrote of the new mission near the Santa Ana mountains. Then, within a matter of days, they stopped the work, buried the two bells and left. Mission San Diego had been attacked, a priest killed. The founding party returned to the presidio.

One year later, Serra traveled to the site of Mission San Juan Capistrano and performed the rituals of a second founding on November 1, 1776. By the time he returned in 1778, the mission had been moved southwest to its present location on a hill with a view to the sea and near three creeks.

The necessities for sustaining life at the new mission came from other missions in the chain. San Diego and San Gabriel donated cows, mules and provisions. Vestments for the priests could be found; carpets and candlesticks could be sent with the ships from Mexico. Mission San Juan Capistrano did get two priests, some soldiers, a

A visitor standing on this paved path in the Central Courtyard, left, looks toward the Fountain of the Four Evangelists and the south wing of the quadrangle, where priests and visitors were housed. Look closely and you'll see that the spaces between the columns of the arches vary — mission builders had no sophisticated measuring devices to ensure uniformity.

Many original mission tiles, right, were reset during various periods of restoration. The structure atop the roof is a capped chimney.

branding iron, 12 hoes, six machetes, two axes, and six knives. With fewer hand tools than a present-day landscaping crew, the priests, the soldiers, and the native people began their mission.

THE CONSTRUCTION

California dirt provided the primary mission building material, adobe for the walls, up to 5 feet thick. Fired, the dirt became bricks for the arches and later for the aqueduct system. Roof tiles were made of clay. Contrary to folklore, the thousands of tiles were not molded across the thighs of the workers but on forms, possibly logs. Some of these tiles still cover the roofs of the mission, having been reset during various periods of restoration. In some rooms, the original ceilings of reeds and mud plaster can still be seen. According to mission archaeologist Harry Francisco, building began on the new site before the permanent move. One of the first structures would have been a little brush chapel.

Buildings and walls went up, forming a Central Courtyard. The resulting quadrangle has four unequal sides. The arches of the surrounding arcades also have varied

African lilies, above and right, float in the Fountain of the Four Evangelists. The bell tower helps distinguish the north wing.

Juaneño artistry is exemplified in their basketry, below.

measurements. Lacking sophisticated tools, the priests had to depend on a critical eye and their feet. They paced the patio, and the arcades followed.

Now viewed as graceful and symbolic architectural elements of the mission style, the covered arcades served an important purpose. The very practical adobe blocks had one great enemy, water. The roofs of the arcade kept the rain from reducing adobe walls to their original state, mud.

The buildings had to meet the needs of the population to be housed. To the south, they built a barracks for the mission soldiers a suitable distance from the dorm for the unmarried women and girls. The complex included kitchens, storerooms, work areas, and a hospital. The two priests assigned to the mission had their living quarters, and visitors had their rooms.

Building a mission did not generally appeal to the Spanish soldiers. Father Lasuén reported a mutinous atmosphere when they were initially told to begin building the new mission. He wrote that he took various steps to appease them, including "training guns on them and bringing them to bear on the barracks." The priests had only one dependable workforce with which the mission could be built and maintained, the Juaneño.

THE BUILDERS

When the Portolá expedition arrived in 1769, an estimated 3,000 to 4,000 Juaneño lived on the land that would become part of the mission. Belonging to the Shoshone linguistic family, they were small in stature and dark-skinned. They lived in communities, building their round homes, *kit'chas*, of reeds, *tules*. They went into the sea to fish in reed canoes sealed with tar. The land provided as well, in the good years supplying them with game and acorns. They expressed their artistry in their baskets.

"A peaceful people," says David Belardes, a descendent of the Juaneño and the Spanish. "More curious. They had no fear."

"They were incredible," says fellow Juaneño descendent Jacque Nunez.

Spanish sources of the period describe the Juaneño as friendly and gentle. They seemed not only interested in the new religion presented to them by the Spanish but also anxious to join. Father Palóu wrote in 1787 that at other missions the native people wanted trinkets, but at Mission San Juan Capistrano they made "repeated requests for baptism."

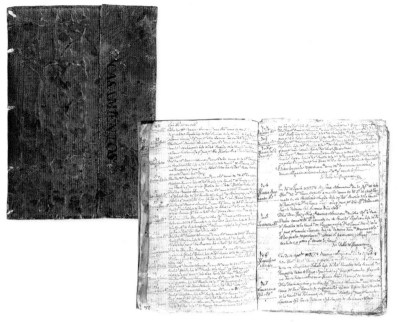

In part, their ancient belief system may account for this. Father Gerónimo Boscana arrived at the mission in 1814 and began to record the traditions and beliefs of the Juaneño. He wrote of the Juaneño deity Chinigchinich, whom they believed came to Earth to teach them, to show them how to live and raise their children in the correct way. He told them, "When I die, I shall ascend above to the stars, and from thence, I shall always see you." The Juaneño also believed a single God created the world, making the first man and woman out of clay.

The first Juaneño baptism took place on December 19, 1776, that of the boy Nanagibar. He would be known from that moment on as Juan Bautista and become a sponsor for many others joining the new religion. The first marriage united Saturnino and Brigida in January 1777, with the first death coming in July, that of the girl Sinforosa. The names can still be read as they were recorded in the sacramental registers given to the mission by Serra and signed with his distinctive flourish.

The Juaneño did many things very well. States mission archaeologist Francisco, "There's just an incredible amount of things that they had to learn, and they did them."

In addition to the building of a mission, they worked

Masonry structures with tiled roofs, stone pathways, and a variety of plantings come together to form a place that invites artists, photographers, and visitors seeking a quiet moment.

Mission archives contain sacramental registers signed by Father Serra, above. Volunteers continue to translate the registers to provide descendants of the Juaneño and Spanish residents with the history of their family lines.

Three arches rest on one pillar where the east and south wings meet. The scene above shows the arcade alongside the Serra Chapel. At right, the foliage is in a corner of the Central Courtyard.

iron, farmed, tended large herds of livestock. They not only learned the art of weaving, they out-wove their instructor.

The priests of San Juan Capistrano paid a master weaver to travel from Monterey in 1796 to show the neophytes how it should be done.

"In no way does it meet our expectations," they wrote of the resulting work of the weaver. But they did note the Juaneño could produce equal, even better, material, and they also knew how to use dyes.

The cloth has long since disappeared. Of the Juaneño baskets made after contact with the Spanish, only a few dozen are known to exist today. The man who may have been the last full-blooded Juaneño, José de Gracia Cruz, or Acu, died in 1924.

In 1993, the state of California officially recognized the existence of the Juaneño, the Acjachemen Nation. Federal recognition has not yet come to those who know they descended from the people who greeted the emissaries of empire and religion and gave them gifts.

TWO CHURCHES TO SERVE

THE GREAT STONE CHURCH

Bostonian Alfred Robinson wrote of massive ruins of a church he saw during his travels in California in 1829. "It still bears the appearance of having been one of the best finished structures of the country and the workmanship displayed in the sculpture upon its walls and its vaulted roof would command admiration in our own country."

The ruins, the Great Stone Church of Mission San Juan Capistrano, still have travelers nodding their heads in respect and experts shaking theirs in wonder. As John Loomis, preservation architect for the mission stated, "If we built it now the way it is built, it would collapse. It is a miracle it's still standing."

In 1797, work began on a new church to replace the mission's small adobe church. A master mason had been requested from Mexico to direct the work, but until he arrived the priests would be in charge — Father Vicente Fustér and Father Juan Norberto de Santiago. They must have had a grand vision of what a church should be, a strong, cathedral-like edifice built of stone in the European way they would have known from their childhoods.

For the walls they used sandstone taken from a quarry believed to be about 2 miles to the east. The stones weighed up to 600 pounds and had to be carted, carried, hauled to the site, then hoisted, pushed, pulled into position.

For the arches, windows, and domes, the builders used limestone, a stronger and better construction material than sandstone but limited in quantity. Softer volcanic tuff was used for carved decorative elements like keystones and pilasters. Although the exact quarry sites for both have not been confirmed, they too were miles from the mission.

The men of the mission moved these mountains of rock. And, according to a mission tale retold by historian Father Zephyrin Engelhardt in his 1922 book *Mission San Juan Capistrano, The Jewel of the Missions*, the women and children asked to help as well.

"Father," they asked, "will small stones be wanted in the great building?"

The results of their contributions can be seen between the boulders, thousands upon thousands of small stones. These chinking stones were pounded in to level the great stones and to fill in the mortar between them. And so the

Viewed here from the Entry Courtyard, above, the ruins of the Great Stone Church are laced with scaffolds on which conservators carry out their efforts to stop further deterioration of the structure brought down by an earthquake in 1812. The bell wall was built after the earthquake.

The earthquake and erosion, opposite page, left the Great Stone Church in ruins, but its spirit remains intact. Shown is the top one-third of the west wall of the church's nave, its long, central portion. An actor stood at the base of this wall in an execution scene in a 1927 movie (see Page 65).

A setting sun casts a golden glow, opposite page, on a portion of the interior east wall of the Great Stone Church's nave. The dome-topped niches about midway up the wall on the left and right sides of the photo once held statues. The church's builders created square recesses, such as those below the arches on the photo's left side, to hold scaffolding as they raised the wall.

This painting by Fred Behre and John Gutzon Borglum, below right, shows Mission San Juan Capistrano and the Great Stone Church before the earthquake. He painted it in 1894, when it was believed that the tower was at the front of the church. Contemporary studies indicate that the tower probably was off to the east side. The snapshot, below left, was taken in the 1890s.

MISSION SAN JUAN CAPISTRANO
FOUNDED 1776
DESTROYED BY EARTHQUAKE 1

walls went up, double walls, the interior of each filled with rubble and mortar.

Father Fustér died in 1800. They buried him in the adobe church. That year the master mason Isidro Aguilar arrived. Three years later he died. The building continued.

The church was designed in the form of a Latin cross, the crossbar forming the transept. Three domes ran the length of the church, the nave; three across the transept; and one over the sanctuary, the altar area. The sacristy, the room to the west of the altar, had a small, almost flat, dome. The approximate length of the church from front door to altar wall was 166 feet 9 inches. The width of the transept measured 84 feet 8 inches. The church may have reached a height of more than 60 feet at the top of the largest dome. Using their brains, their backs, and a bare minimum of tools, the people of the mission had created the largest man-made structure west of the Mississippi River.

Religious art would have adorned the interior, with statues of the saints housed in niches, nine on the wall behind the altar. Designs were carved on the stones around the domes, possibly artistic representations of local plant life. The traces of the colors remain, faded green and soft red. The flower pattern of the keystone of the sanctuary

dome can still be seen. A beige-colored lime mortar, still visible, covered the walls.

The floor of the church may have been packed dirt with a finish of diamond-shaped tiles beginning near the altar. No pews in this church, no seats to cushion the hours that the faithful knelt on the floor. The four bells that called them to their prayers rang from the bell tower. Speculation continues over the height and the position of that tower.

No drawings of the church are known to exist. In 1894, an artist did a re-creation of the entire mission complex showing the bell tower at the front of the church. That positioning lasted in source material until the last decades of the 20TH century. However, contemporary archaeological studies indicate that the tower stood on the east side of the church.

Estimates of the height vary wildly. Some believe the tower may have reached more than 100 feet. One historian had it at 125 feet, extremely high for the period and possibly too high to be aesthetically complementary to the church. More conservative calculations now place the height at 60 to 65 feet, still tall and possibly too thin. Does it matter? Ah, yes, the tower would matter.

Completed in 1806, the church was dedicated with

A statue of St. Teresa of Avila, left, graces a small altar of the church where Father Serra said Mass. The book she holds symbolizes her extensive writings on religion and the religious life. She founded the order of the Descalced (barefoot) Carmelites in the 1560s.

An ornate altarpiece, background, graces an otherwise simple church called the Serra Chapel. Much of the art and statuary dates to the mission period.

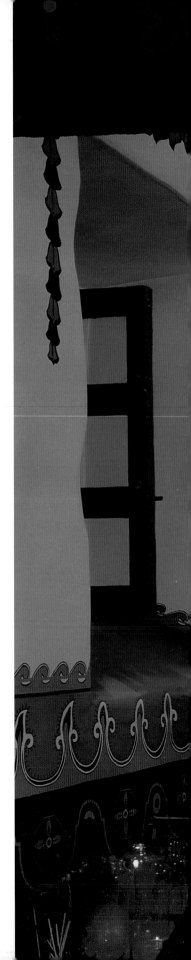

much festivity. The body of the priest who had led the construction, Father Fustér, was reburied near the altar. Neither the joy of accomplishment nor the grave would last long. On Sunday morning, December 8, 1812, an earthquake rolled across California and down the line of missions including Santa Clara de Asís, San Buenaventura, La Purísima Concepción de Maria Santísima, Santa Inés, Santa Barbara, San Gabriel, and Mission San Juan Capistrano where people were gathered for the first service of the day.

With an estimated strength of 8.2 on the Richter scale, the earthquake sent many running for the west door of the church, which today would have opened onto the paths of the rose garden. The tremor had jammed the door shut. The tall, thin bell tower begun to sway, once, twice. Then, the two bell ringers within, the tower crashed in a diagonal line across the roof, reaching to that door where the people huddled. Forty died. The priest, Father José Barona, entered the names of the dead in the burial register, the same book in which his own name would be written 19 years later.

With the Great Stone Church in ruins, the people and the priests of Mission San Juan Capistrano returned to the little adobe church. The body of Father Fustér also made the return trip.

SERRA CHAPEL

They still go to the adobe church every Sunday morning: men, women, children, family groups. They make a small parade down *El Camino Real*, entering the mission through a side gate, walking the path beneath a drapery of red bougainvillea. They arrive early for the 8 o'clock Mass because the church will be, as always, full.

The women cover their heads, in the old way, with scarves, hats, and mantillas. The priest says the Mass in the old way, in Latin, facing the altar, not the congregation. The children, in the very old way, sit sweetly quiet.

This church, a simple rectangle measuring 100 feet 3 inches in length, 27 feet 3 inches in width, and 29 feet high, remains solidly linked to the past. Father Serra led services here in 1778 and 1783. Much of the art and statuary is original to the mission period, to this church, and to the Great Stone Church. Altar pieces, including candlesticks, silver missal stand, and altar card frames have been part of the mission since its early years. The banister in the choir loft had been the altar rail in the Great Stone Church.

A motif of navy blue, moss green, and soft crimson decorates the 4-foot-thick adobe walls. Patterns of flowers,

Serra Chapel has undergone a number of additions and restorations. In the 1920s, right, the ceiling was raised to accommodate a new altar. Here, the chapel's east side is viewed from an area that includes the church's cemetery (not shown).

A statue of Father Serra stands beneath the pulpit in the small church that still serves the faithful and attracts tens of thousands of visitors each year. The large painting on the wall represents the 12TH Station of the Cross, the crucified Christ.

geometric diamonds cut by crosses and leaf-tipped vines, wind through the church and across the beamed ceiling. Restorers working in the 1920s re-created the designs from existing art and from designs found in other missions in the chain.

Fourteen Stations of the Cross, the visual depictions of Christ's path to the Crucifixion, hang on the walls. Unsigned, dark and somber as their subject, 13 of them predate the mission. A 20TH century copy of the massive oil painting by artist José Francisco Zervas of the death of Christ hangs as the 12TH station, covering the damaged original. But the most startling art of the chapel, the work that demands the upward gaze, the stare, does not hang on a wall. This piece of art creates a wall.

In 1906, the Diocese of Los Angeles received a gift of a golden altar and reredos, the ornamental wood altarpiece. Made in Barcelona, Spain, the baroque altar probably dates from the mid-1600s, the time of the Manchu dynasty in China, the building of Versailles in France, and the completion of the Taj Mahal in India. The size and gold leaf glow of the carved cherry wood seemed fitting for nothing less than a cathedral. Waiting for the right place and a willing pastor, the altar went into storage, forgotten.

Then, in the early 1920s a priest came forward who knew the perfect spot for the grandiose work. Father St. John O'Sullivan of Mission San Juan Capistrano did not have a cathedral, but he had no doubts about the stature of his own church. In 1922, the Golden Altar went to the church where Serra had served. The priest wrote of the arrival with the enthusiasm of someone who has made a great find.

"Before I got it, it was offered to others, but rejected as 'no good,' — an old worm-eaten thing . . . Never mind, when it is up and in the setting we will give it, somebody will be sorry." But before a covetous glance would be given, they had to put the masterpiece together.

The altar and reredos came as a puzzle, 10 crates, and 396 pieces of pillars, niches, arches, curlicues, angels, and saints. Once united, they would present another poser. The Golden Altar loomed bigger than the church. The sides had to be cut to fit within the old walls. To accommodate the altar's height of 22-1/2 feet, the ceiling of the church had to be raised 8 feet. It still looks like a tight fit for the figure of God that sits at the very top, one hand holding the universe, the other raised in a blessing, his head almost grazing the roof.

Below God, an angel sails downward over the ornate

In the beginning, there was God, the Creator, depicted at topmost center of the Golden Altar, opposite page. In the center is the Crucifix.

Other depictions include, on the upper tier, from left: St. Peter, the fisherman, the apostle chosen by Christ to lead the Church. The key he holds is to the kingdom of Heaven.

San Juan Capistrano (1386-1456), who was an Italian lawyer and governor before joining the Franciscans. He successfully led an army against invaders at the Battle of Belgrade when he was 70.

St. Michael the Archangel, who is armed with a sword with which he leads spiritual armies in fighting evil.

On the lower tier, from left: St. Francis of Assisi (circa 1182-1226), who is the founder of the Order of Friars Minor, generally called the Franciscans. Appearing with symbols of animals and birds, he is the patron saint of animals and ecologists.

Virgin of Guadalupe, who appeared before Juan Diego in Mexico in December 1531. The painting depicts the imprint that she left on Juan Diego's cloak. This depiction of Christ's mother is especially revered in Mexico.

St. Clare of Assisi (circa 1193-1253). She holds a monstrance, the vessel used in exposition of the Blessed Sacrament, the transformation of Christ's body into a wafer of bread. An Italian noble, she entered the religious life in 1212 as a result of St. Francis's preaching. She founded the order of nuns called Poor Clares, pledged to absolute poverty.

At bottom center of the lower portion of the altar is the Sacred Heart of Christ.

Above, one of the many angels of the Golden Altar graces an arch beneath the painting of the Virgin of Guadalupe.

ST. PEREGRINE'S CHAPEL

gold leaf swirls. Other angels, more than 50 of them, peer out with wise, chubby faces from the reredos and peek from around the golden fruit-on-the-vine-encircled golden pillars.

Carved wood figures representing saints of the Catholic Church sit in the niches. Some are original to the altar; others were carved after the altar arrived. As shown in the photograph on Page 42, San Juan Capistrano stands below the God figure in the upper tier, with St. Peter holding the key to the kingdom of Heaven to the viewer's left. To the viewer's right, St. Michael the Archangel triumphs over evil with one foot firmly planted on the dragon's head.

The painting of the Virgin of Guadalupe, original to the mission, holds the position of honor in the center niche of the lower tier, with St. Francis of Assisi, founder of the Franciscan order, to the viewer's left, and St. Clare, founder of the Poor Sisters of Clare, on the right.

The statue of St. Joseph, protector of the young Christ, stands on the left side of the altar; saint and writer Teresa of Avila holds book and pen on the right. And, while the men of his order may have been exiled from the empire, St. Ignatius Loyola, founder of the Jesuit order, has a home here next to the pulpit. St. Dominic, founder of the Dominican order, stands on the opposite wall.

One of the statues begs to be touched, St. Peregrine. The patron saint of those suffering from cancer has his own shrine on the east side of the chapel, a tiny room of hope for those who despair. Candles symbolizing the offered prayers flicker before the kneeling statue of the saint. Other prayers have been written out, the tiny pieces of paper tightly rolled and squeezed within the marble crevasses of the statue. Gold can also be found in this simple room, in the light of those candles.

The church maintains a sense of the sacred. People, full of the excitement of the day outside, go silent as they come into the church. A few pause at the doorway to St. Peregrine's shrine, a few enter. Some slide into the pews of the church to sit or kneel. The faithful have never really left the old walls and the old ways of Serra Chapel. But, as with the Golden Altar, sometimes you just have to raise the roof.

BASILICA DE SAN JUAN CAPISTRANO

By the 1980s, the Catholic population of the town of San Juan Capistrano and surrounding communities had far outgrown the walls of Serra Chapel.

A five-year building project resulted in the Basilica of San Juan Capistrano on the immediate northwest corner of the mission complex. The design of the basilica replicates that of the Great Stone Church, though about 30 percent larger in scale. This bell tower stands at 109 feet.

As would have been the case with the Great Stone Church, everything about the basilica seems monumental. The towering walls topped by domes dwarf the human figure. The largest dome weighs more than 10 tons. Enormous designs of garlands of flowers and vases decorate the walls in vivid colors. The late California mission art historian Dr. Norman Neuerburg designed the folk art decor based on what existed in the interior of the Great Stone Church.

The parish of 6,000 members includes many of the Spanish-speaking people of the area, be they new arrivals or old. They fill the church for the Spanish Mass every Sunday afternoon. They line the walls, move in the aisles, go in and out the doors. Here, children laugh, sometimes cry, in the spirit of a family of worshippers.

The Basilica of San Juan Capistrano, flanking the northwestern edge of the mission quadrangle, copies the Great Stone Church but exceeds it in size.

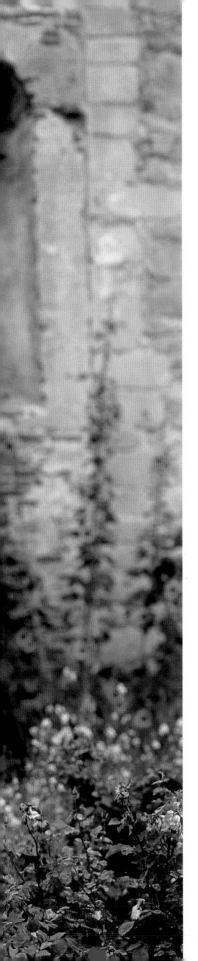

MISSION BELLS

Bells were integrated into daily mission life, calling the faithful to daily events. On the opposite page, the bell wall, called the *campanario*, holds two of the Great Stone Church's original bells – the smaller ones – and two replicas cast from molds made from the originals.

Viewed from the Entry Courtyard, the bell wall, right, was built in about 1813, after an earthquake left the church in ruins. The wall with a cross atop it was built even later.

THE QUARTET

Four bells once rang from the tower of the Great Stone Church. They came to the mission with names and messages. San Vicente, the largest, announced in an inscription that he had been cast in 1796 in honor of the two priests at the mission, Father Fustér and Father Santiago. The next in size proclaimed, "Ruelas made me and I call myself San Juan." San Juan also had the birth date of 1796. The two smaller bells, San Antonio and San Rafael, cast in 1804, carried the inscriptions of their dedication to the Virgin Mary.

Now, the *campanario*, the bell wall, houses the mission bells. The two small bells are original. The two larger ones are copies, the originals replaced in 2001 because of cracks.

"Not the same sound," commented Michael Gastelum of the new arrivals. He rings the bells of the mission as did his grandfather before him, Paul "Mocho" Arbiso. He and others of the mission remember a time when the bells would ring to mark morning, noon, and evening. He remembers their songs.

"The way they were tolled you knew if a woman died or if a man died," he says. And, when a child died, the little bells, "angel bells," he explains, would make the call.

Today, the sound of the bells has been re-created by technology. A tape plays at the mission to mark the hours with peals and bell music. A computer directs the ringing of the basilica's eight bells at noon, 6 P.M., and for Mass. But, the bells of the *campanario* ring only on special occasions. Sometimes a visitor might be granted the privilege of pulling the nylon cords. That would not have happened in the old days.

In the 1880s, a sailor came to the mission town on a one-man liberty. His revel led him to the mistake, if joyous, of ringing the mission bells. Roused from their beds, the townspeople marched to the mission and gave the man a sound thrashing. Their bells, the bells of all the missions, demanded respect. They once controlled the schedule of life.

MISSION DAYS

Both people and bells sang out at the beginning of each day at the mission. The people sang the morning hymn, which began *"Ya viene el alba,"* (Now

The Sacred Garden, left and opposite page, is nestled behind the bell wall, offering a place that invites visitors to stay for a while and wonder about all the people the bells have summoned and all the events they have heralded. The garden's arched entry was completed in 1918, when the garden was called the Hidden Garden and Garden of the Bells. The large bell at right is named after San Vicente, a copy of a bell dating to 1796.

comes the dawn). The bell called for the religious service followed by a breakfast of *atole*, a hot cereal made of toasted grain. Then, the workday began.

The mission's western wing took on the activity of an 18TH century industrial park. Women scraped cowhides for the fat to make candles and soap. They wove baskets and cloth. Men worked the brick furnaces producing the iron. They made furniture, adobes, and tiles.

Women in the kitchen stayed busy with the constant preparation of the three mission meals for a population of more than 1,000. The pantries stored meat from the mission herds, olive oil pressed in the mission's mill, grains from the fields, and vegetables and fruits from the gardens and orchards. The land proved bountiful, as did the vines.

Mission San Juan Capistrano may have been the first in California to produce wine. Vine cuttings were sent up from Mexico in 1778. One of the brick vats at the mission winery could hold an estimated 5,000 gallons of wine.

Mission fields yielded crops of grain and corn. The records for 1784 show a total harvest of more than 3,000 bushels of wheat, corn, and beans. By 1810, the harvest reached 5,892 bushels, and eight years later, 14,562 bushels. The grazing land proved no less productive. The mission had 703 head of cattle in 1784. By 1810, nearly 10,000 head roamed the approximately 200,000 acres controlled by the mission. More than 11,000 sheep grazed the hills. In 1796 the mission sent more than 3,000 pounds of wool to Mission Santa Barbara.

"It was the most prosperous mission of all of them," firmly states archaeologist Francisco.

The work that made that possible came to a halt with the midday bell and a meal of *pozole*, a stew of meat and vegetables. After a break, work resumed until the ringing of the bell at sunset and the call to another hot meal. One traveler to the northern missions of California estimated the size of one serving of the mission stew at 1-1/2 quarts. The day ended with a few free hours and then bed.

The two resident priests had their own schedules to keep, which included care of the sick and the elderly, teaching, oversight of the work of the community, attending to spiritual needs, and paperwork. They wrote meticulous reports and inventories. All had to be copied a second time, perhaps a third, for their own records.

Soldiers made up the third component of the mission's residents. Called *soldados de cuero*, "leatherjackets," because of their leather armor, never more than a dozen

48

served at the mission. No more than 300 served the entire mission chain and the four presidios. California did not offer much of an opportunity for a military man. Soldiers found themselves far from the seat of power and the sources of promotion. They couldn't depend on their pay with supply ships arriving months late, if at all. Once paid, what could they buy?

Festivals and holy days did break the humdrum of the regimented mission life, as did music. Mission San Juan Capistrano, along with others in the chain, had a band or an orchestra. The instruments may have included violins, flutes, violas, horns, and guitars, some made in Europe, others made at the missions. The people of the mission also had music in their voices, singing the music of the services. But, try to break through the regimentation in ways other than those prescribed by mission life and punishment could follow. Infractions included leaving a mission without permission and not doing the assigned labor. Transgressors could be whipped, held in stocks, or forced to work with an iron chain or rod around one leg.

Corporal punishment was standard to the period and to the government, military, and religious institutions. As late as 1672, those accused of heresy or blasphemy under the Spanish Inquisition received up to 200 lashes. One hundred fifty years later, sailors, including those on ships flying the red, white, and blue flag of the new nation to the east, were flogged until their backs were a bloody mess.

Overt abuses of power within mission systems through the Spanish empire resulted in rebellions by the native workers. One beating administered by a soldier at the California Mission Santa Inés brought on a major revolt against a number of missions in 1824.

The written history of Mission San Juan Capistrano does not mention incidents of rebellion. One reason may be found in those full storage rooms: dependable, abundant food. In the creation of that food supply, the need for the old ways of hunting and gathering on the land had disappeared, as had the game. The native economy ended with establishment of mission life.

VISITORS

Reports on daily life at the missions of California came from those who sailed and rode the coast. Some made the trip for adventure, others strictly for profit. A rich mission, or a poor one, had things to sell.

The western side of the mission was devoted to producing products used day-to-day at the mission and for trade with the crews of ships anchored off the nearby coast. Above from left are the remains of a foundry, rendering pots for making soap and candles, and an olive mill.

The mission priests had things they needed to buy. In the years of the empire, trading was officially restricted to Spanish vessels but unofficially open to all.

Artifacts discovered at Mission San Juan Capistrano show the mission did have contact with the products of the world. Shards of plate ware have been discovered, including those of English, North American, and Chinese origin. The ships that stopped, Spanish and others, would be interested in what the mission produced in quantity: hides and beef, and tallow, the rendered fat used for candles and soap. The mission would have been interested in obtaining some of the staples and the luxuries of life its workshops and gardens could not provide. Ships carried carpets, vestments, fabrics, foodstuffs, hardware, pig iron for iron working, and spices for cooking.

One of the visitors brought by the sea had no plans for the balanced give and take of trade. He came strictly for the taking, from other ships and from the missions. Argentine revolutionary and pirate Hippolyte de Bouchard arrived on the coast in 1818. He sacked Monterey and moved south. At Mission San Juan Capistrano he demanded supplies. The mission population headed for the hills, carrying with them the valuables of the church. They left the pirates to

the mission and the mission wine.

For three days, the pirates enjoyed the fermented fruit of the vine. Then, the local story goes, they reeled back to the beach, some so drunk or sick they had to be tied to their own cannons.

Richard Dana, the author of *Two Years Before the Mast*, made a far less rambunctious stop on the beach below the mission in 1835. Having left Harvard and Boston because of an eye problem, he signed on the brig *Pilgrim* as a common sailor and set sail for California.

The *Pilgrim* and other ships making the long voyage around Cape Horn were part of the hide trade. The hides of tens of thousands of head of California mission cattle could be turned into cash. Carried back to American ports, they would become boots and shoes and all the leather trappings necessary to a horse-drawn civilization.

By the end of the mission era in the 1830s, a hide sold for $1 to $2.50. They became the local currency, earning the nickname, "California banknotes." The ships would ply the coastline until they had as many as 40,000 hides stored below, only then leaving for the harrowing trip back around the Horn. Dana's book recounted his experiences in the trade and introduced the English-speaking world to California

This bronze statue at Dana Point, not far from the mission, depicts a muscled sailor tossing a cowhide. In the 1800s hides from mission cattle were flung into the ocean where the crews of waiting ships picked them up for transport to leather markets.

and to a place called San Juan Capistrano.

He saw the slice of the beach and the green hills beyond it, and pronounced, "San Juan is the only romantic spot in California." He and his shipmates also saw a rock wall rising more than 200 feet high from the beach. The hides waited on the other side, stiff, folded in half, bulky, heavy. How would they get them down with the minimum amount of time and effort? They threw them. The resulting vision held its own romance.

Dana wrote, ". . . the wind took them, and they swayed and eddied about, plunging and rising in the air, like a kite when it has broken its string."

A life-sized statue of a brawny, bare chested, barefoot sailor now stands atop the cliffs. He moves in a bronze twist, swinging a hide high into the air. Below, modern-day sailing craft sparkle in a white-on-blue marina not far from where Dana found a peace he had not known since leaving home.

". . . and I experienced a glow of pleasure at finding that what of poetry and romance I ever had in me, had not been entirely deadened by the laborious and frittering life I had led."

Richard Dana returned to Harvard and the study of law. Unfortunately, he never wrote of any visit to the old mission on the hill, but another visitor would when recounting his own travels in California. He too would create a vision.

". . . stopped a while at the mission which is close by the river," wrote adventurer, traveler, and author H.M.T. Powell of his 1850 visit to Mission San Juan Capistrano. "With difficulty took a slight sketch, rain hindered me from taking a good one." His would be the first known drawing of the mission.

 # THE ART
OF THE GARDENS

"Look at the garden, how pretty," a woman calls out as she enters the mission. Yellow roses the size of cabbages rise from the garden to meet her.

"I don't think the gardens in this place have ever been prettier than they are today," comments a man standing by an easel. He uses his art to capture the way the waterfall of purple bougainvillea flows across the corner of the bell wall.

They see what the earlier visitors to this mission never saw, the planned and cultivated splendor of the gardens. Prior to the 20TH century, what grew at the mission had one basic purpose, to feed the population. The peach, apricot, and pomegranate trees might turn the springtime orchards into a pastel paradise, but the fruit that followed had the real value. The mission's Central Courtyard would have been equally basic, dirt.

As stated by Jerry Sortomme, head of the Environmental Horticulture Program at Santa Barbara Community College and researcher of mission era plants, "I think aesthetics proved to be a pure luxury at that time."

Flowers did have a place at this and other missions, for use on the altar. Perhaps the mission had a few pots of flowers and some flowering plants within the grounds, but if not, the land again provided. White poppies flourished

In season, lilies highlight a garden alongside the arcade flanking the Serra Chapel in the southeast corner of the Central Courtyard.

Artist Colin Campbell Cooper depicted aesthetic and functional mission elements in a painting he named *Mission San Juan Capistrano*. The work, dated 1916, remains a part of the mission's art collection.

Mission gardens thrive with the work of volunteers called the Gardening Angels and without the use of chemical pesticides. The gardens grow as works in progress, colors and plant types changing with the seasons. The views above are, from left, from the Entry Courtyard, looking toward the North Wing from the West Wing, and looking northwest from the Central Courtyard.

A colorful display of roses, opposite page, greets visitors as they pass through the front gate and into the Entry Courtyard.

around Mission San Juan Capistrano — and lavender-hued wild hyacinths and native yellow violas. Wild roses grew. Serra had noted this flower when he entered California, proclaiming it the flower of his own land, the rose of Castile. This rose of California now grows in the mission gardens, a small path of pink, quite dainty when considering the riotous splash of its nearby cousins.

Roses fill the entry gardens, their colors punctuating the air. The Sterling Silver has gone mauve, the petals of the Double Delight move from deep pink to yellow, the Iceberg stays white, the Sweet Inspiration girl-baby pink, and the Elena sunshine yellow.

A flock of birds of paradise, spiked neon purple, like the coiffure statements of another generation, stands almost eye-high with the visitors coming into the garden. Deeper and calmer purple morning glories form a canopy over the ramada where people sit and admire. Those visitors who are even closer to the ground and the flowers have their own place to visit, almost a secret, and very, very small.

The Children's Garden has flowers and plants that look like pincushions, and fan-tailed shrimp, and a mouse, and all just the right size for little wanderers. The long-limbed kangaroo paws reach into their imaginations while

they reach out to the fuzzy-leafed green lamb's ear and the nutmeg-smelling geraniums. In their garden, should they wish to sit and admire, a tiny chair awaits.

Outside, in the other gardens, the giants live. The trees of the mission range from the massive pepper trees in the Entry Courtyard to the palms, which have the audacity to outreach the remaining dome of the Great Stone Church. Jacarandas grow above the arches of the Central Courtyard, becoming lacey purple fans against the sky in early summer.

The gardens began in 1910 with the arrival of Father St. John O'Sullivan. During his 23 years as pastor, he would be instrumental in the rebirth of the mission after a long period of decay. Using local workers and laborers who just happened by the mission, he ended the strictly utilitarian use of the gardens. Flowers and trees were planted, and fountains installed. Art and photography of the period captured the transition from that dirt-filled courtyard of 1900 to the roses and meandering paths of 1924.

Paul Arbiso, descendent of the Juaneño and bell ringer for the mission, also tended the mission gardens under O'Sullivan. He remained in the gardens until his death in 1994 at age 99. A plaque honoring him hangs in yet another garden, the secluded Sacred Garden formed by the wall of

An artistic mix of textures, shapes, and shadows first attracted artists to Mission San Juan Capistrano in the 1880s. The later addition of gardens imbued the mission with a new vibrancy. Looking across one side of a pond in the Entry Courtyard, a visitor sees the south side of the South Wing.

This mélange of plants and flowers, left, comes together into a splendid scene for those with an artistic eye. The painting, opposite page, shows the south side of the South Wing. Artist Kevin Kibsey titled his 2001 oil *Mission Courtyard with Pepper Tree*, a reference to a huge tree dating to the 1880s.

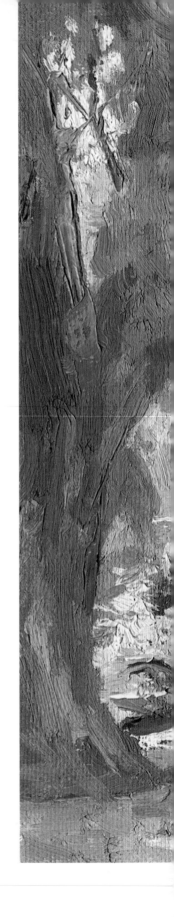

the bells and one wall of the Great Stone Church.

In Genesis, God created a garden. At Mission San Juan Capistrano, the angels decided to help . . . on Wednesdays.

They call themselves the Gardening Angels. In 1997 this volunteer group formed to tend the mission gardens. Every Wednesday morning they appear, trowels at the ready, to plant, weed, mumble at, wrestle with, move around, and love the flowers and plants of the mission. They use no pesticides other than natural horticultural oil mixed with water. They use an organic, humus-based fertilizer. Three to four times a year they mulch with a dump truck load of a compost made of redwood, Douglas fir, and the always very organic horse manure.

The result of their dedication and that of the staff gardeners and landscapers has earned national recognition. Thousands of people make a trip to the mission for the annual June flower and garden show. But, the gardeners aren't the only ones busy among the trees and flowers of the mission. Other artists work beside them, the painters.

"I was just overwhelmed by the beauty of the place," commented Arizona-based artist Kevin Kibsey. "I didn't know what to paint first." In six days at the mission, he produced 10 oil paintings in the plein air style of sit, cap-

ture the light and beauty of the moment, the hour, and then you must be done.

Playing with the light and shadows of the day, the walls of the mission offer up a rich palette of colors: cream moving to beige to dusty gold, with reddish undertones turning to pink. The imperfection of the broken layers of mortar upon adobe and brick reach perfection when translated in oil and watercolor. The mission mesmerizes artists, and has for a long time.

They arrived in the 1880s, men and women with artistic ties to the great cities of the Midwest and the East Coast. The world of art was on the move as well, the impressionists of Paris of the 1870s leading the way. The mission, crumbling and all but abandoned, presented an exotic subject. They painted the arcades that seemed to end with an arch suspended in mid air. They painted sheep grazing in the courtyard. The bells, the Great Stone Church in the moonlight, the people still practicing the faith, all became subjects for their talent.

But, set up an easel and you are bound to find a critic looking over your shoulder.

"We watch misguided persons sitting around and perpetuating horrors in red and nightmares in green under

the name of water-colors," wrote Adeline Stearns Wing, in the *Land of Sunshine* magazine in 1895.

She mused, "Would that one of our great artists would come and do justice to the most picturesque ruins in the United States." She should have introduced herself. The greats of California art and the art of the country were already there. John Gutzon Borglum, creator of the presidential images sculpted onto Mount Rushmore, and artist Elizabeth Borglum, his wife, painted at San Juan Capistrano in the 1890s, as did Fannie E. Duvall. Elmer Wachtel worked day and night at the mission. Colin Campbell Cooper painted the mission, as did William Wendt, and Alson S. Clark.

And, when the gardening began, when the flowers grew, and the fountains played, they painted the gardens. Joseph Kleitsch, one of the founders of the Laguna art colony, first visited the mission in 1913. He retuned to live and paint in California in 1920. Jean Stern, expert in impressionist art pronounced Kleitsch's *San Juan Capistrano* to be "one of the finest impressionist paintings produced in California."

Some artists stayed at the mission, renting rooms for their studios or as guests. Some left works behind as a thank-you. Others left pieces that were purchased. Like

A well used in the mission's early days presides in the centers of these two scenes, which are among the first a visitor sees after coming through the entry gate. The immense pepper tree casts shadows about the courtyard like an artist puts paint to canvas.

the Golden Altar, some of those paintings spent the next decades forgotten until the 1990s, when they were discovered in the basement of one of the mission buildings. They now hang in the administration building.

The mission also provided a scenic backdrop for early California filmmakers. In the 1924 *Mademoiselle Midnight*, the mission became a cattle ranch in Mexico. In *Rose of the Golden West*, 1927, the Great Stone Church became the site of an execution, with actor Gilbert Roland set to die by firing squad.

Director D.W. Griffith pioneered filmdom's use of the mission with his 1910 *Two Brothers*, the first movie made in Orange County. Both Mary Pickford and Mack Sennett had roles. As related by John Sleeper in his book *Great Movies Shot in Orange County*, the filming started with a near-riot.

Townspeople had joined for a funeral procession before the filming began. When Griffith started his first day of work with an enactment of an Easter procession, the still-mourning citizens thought they were being mocked. Once again, they formed ranks and advanced. They attacked the actor playing the priest. Griffith offered an apology in the form of a rodeo put on by his wranglers.

One painting of the mission presents a bit of a mys-tery tied to its popularity as a film setting. American artist Charles Percy Austin painted *Mary Pickford's Wedding* dated 1924, showing the silent movie star and her husband, Owen Moore, leaving the mission chapel in wedding finery. One of the guests depicted, a kind of dark shadow to the right of the canvas, is believed to be director Griffith.

However, Mary Pickford's first marriage to Moore did not take place at that time nor at the mission. She married actor Moore in a 1911 civil ceremony in New Jersey. She went on to marry her second husband, Douglas Fairbanks, in 1920, and her third husband, Buddy Rogers, in 1937, both without a mission in sight. However, there had been yet another marriage. In 1915 Mary Pickford and Owen Moore were joined for a second time, this time in a religious ceremony at Mission San Juan Capistrano. The event was captured in a colorful painting of a day full of people, flowers, and mission walls.

WHEN THE WALLS CAME DOWN

REVOLUTION

The location of the California mission chain at the edge of the empire provided relative isolation from the events of the world beyond. During the years of the chain's growth and prosperity, the flames of rebellion rose in Europe and on the American continent. The first founding of Mission San Juan Capistrano took place in the year of the American Revolution, the second founding in the year of the Declaration of Independence. While the mission buildings rose in 1791, the slaves of the Caribbean Island of Santo Domingo revolted against the French colonizers. Herds of cattle and sheep covered mission land in 1793 while royal heads rolled in Paris.

In 1810 in the town of Dolores in central Mexico, Father Miguel Hidalgo cried out for liberty and Mexico. The reverberations of the *Grito de Dolores* and the rebellion against the Spanish would have a major impact on California, but not quite yet.

The year 1820 proved a good one for Mission San Juan Capistrano, with more than 25,000 cattle, sheep, and horses in the fields. By 1832 the entire mission chain had produced more than four million bushels of agricultural products. Estimates have about 20,000 neophytes attached to the missions during this period, with more than 1,000 at Mission San Juan Capistrano. Then, in 1824, Mexico declared itself a republic and took a hard look north.

Carlos III may have initially missed the true bounty of California, the land, but the new country of Mexico did not. Millions of acres lay under the control of the mission system. Now the cries went up for secularization of the missions, taking control of the land from the church and the Franciscans. In the process and in theory, the native people would become fully self-sufficient, tax-paying citizens.

Perhaps anticipating what actually would transpire, the priests at Mission San Juan Capistrano wrote in 1827 of the natives' rights to the land, declaring ". . . all these lands did belong and do belong to the Indians. On these lands they were born and on them were born likewise all their fathers and all their forefathers." The sentiment would not prevent the inevitable.

Full emancipation of the neophytes came in 1833. In 1834 Mexico began confiscating mission land and property. An inventory placed the value of Mission San Juan

Restoration of Mission San Juan Capistrano had begun a few years earlier when this photo was taken in about 1900. The view is from the south.

Historically known as a sculptor of works of monumental scale— most notably the busts of four presidents on Mount Rushmore in South Dakota, John Gutzon Borglum also painted at the mission. In his 1897 *Sheep Grazing*, opposite page, he presents artistic proof of the years of decay.

This stark vision of decay, left, echoed all along the California mission chain in the late 1880s. The cow grazes in the now-lush Central Courtyard. With decay stopped and a vine added, the same arch presents a resplendent image today.

Capistrano at $54,456. Eight hundred sixty-one neophytes remained at the mission, a figure reduced to 80 only four years later. By then, the once massive cattle herd had decreased to fewer than 500 head.

An enormous land transfer took place throughout California, with great blocks of mission lands going into private hands. Small parcels were earmarked for distribution to the mission Indians. Some of the parcels went unclaimed; others were sold by their Indian owners; and others were lost to new settlers, who used mission neophytes as their own laborers.

Another declaration, this one in 1841, established the pueblo of San Juan Capistrano. The man supervising the division of mission land and property reported the results at the mission as the "complete demoralization of the Indians." And, he added, "it afforded shelter to some knaves . . ." He resigned.

At the *asistencia* of San Antonio de Pala, a small satellite mission of Mission San Luis Rey, a sign in the museum describes this period with the succinct, "Sad days befell Pala." Similar words could have been written on the walls of all the missions.

The priest at Mission San Juan Capistrano wrote his superiors of his stranded situation in a mission that no longer had any wheat, nor wine, and certainly no chocolate. In addition, the appointed government administrator of the once flourishing mission informed him, "He finds no cattle, no sheep, nor anything."

Enter Pio Pico. Born and baptized at Mission San Gabriel, he had deep family roots in the outposts of Spain. His father served as corporal of the San Diego garrison. His aunt married a mason at Mission San Juan Capistrano. In 1843, Pio Pico became governor of California.

As he wrote in a narrative published 80 years after his death, he had a clear understanding of the objective of secularization. That was, "To abolish completely the regime of missions, and to establish pueblos in their place . . ." When his turn at power came, he finished the missions. He sold them.

Mission San Buenaventura went for $12,000 to a man who planned to subdivide the land for new settlers from the United States. The scheme failed. Mission Santa Barbara went for $7,500, Santa Inés for $7,000. San Luis Rey, "The King," fell for $2,437 and San Luis Obispo for a mere $500. As Pico himself admitted, some went "for such an insignificant amount that it makes one ashamed to mention it."

Mission San Juan Capistrano sold for $710 dollars to two men. One, James McKinley, did not stay long enough to figure into the mission's history, but the other, John Forster, moved his family into the mission. An Englishman, Forster arrived in Los Angeles in 1833 and married a daughter of California named Ysidora Pico. Yes, Governor Pico, who made a number of such interesting transactions, sold the jewel of the adobe necklace that had once graced the long coast of California to his brother-in-law.

RUINS

The next wave of politics and power to reach California came from the east. Mexico and the United States went to war in 1846, beginning with a dispute over whether the Rio Grande formed the boundary between the two countries. Gen. Stephen Kearny and the 100-man-strong Army of the West entered California in the fall of that year. In December, he faced California troops under Gen. Andrés Pico, brother of Pio, at the Battle of San Pasqual. Fought 30 miles southeast of the mission, the battle went to the Californios, but one month later Los Angeles fell to American forces.

The war ended with the 1848 Treaty of Guadalupe Hidalgo. Mexico turned over half of its territory, including California, to the United States. The United States, paying a compensation of $15 million, had unknowingly marched into a veritable gold mine. Nine days before the signing of the treaty an unreported discovery of gold had been made in the Sacramento Valley of California. Within a year, a hundred thousand would-be millionaires from around the world headed for California in hopes of finding their own golden future.

The newfound wealth of the territory did not reach the old missions. Reporter J. Ross Browne wrote of his travels in the California of 1849 and of the condition of the missions he visited. At the northern mission of Nuestra Señora de la Soledad he found, "The old church is partially in ruins . . . Not a tree or shrub is to be seen any where in the vicinity."

To the south, Mission San Miguel Arcángel survived as "a motley collection of ruinous old buildings," in a setting "wild and desolate." He described the land between the two missions as plagued with bandits.

Mission San Juan Capistrano fared somewhat better. The presence of a family in residence provided protection

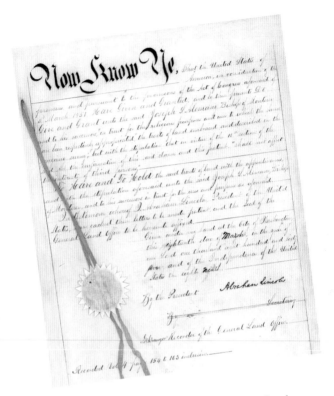

By the early 1920s, tourists were parking their cars outside the newly built south wall. This view across the Entry Courtyard is much the same today, although the huge pepper tree's limbs had not lapped over the wing to the right of it, and more of the Great Stone Church's domes remained.

The document above, signed by President Abraham Lincoln, returned Mission San Juan Capistrano and other missions to the Catholic Church. The document is stored in the mission archives.

against looters and vandalism. Forster also did some repair work on the buildings, but time and nature were bound to win this battle. Without constant maintenance, without sound roofs, the adobe melted, the walls collapsed. An attempt at repairing and rebuilding the Great Stone Church ended in disaster.

Some mission scholars believe that townspeople working on the church in the 1860s decided the remaining domes were unsafe. They used black powder to bring them down with two separate blasts. In Powell's 1850 sketch, at least four domes remained on the church. After the black powder did its work, only two survived, the dome over the sanctuary and the small dome over the sacristy.

The twenty-year residency of the Forster family ended with the signature of President Abraham Lincoln. In 1865, less than a month before his assassination, he signed the papers that officially returned the mission to the Catholic Church. Forster went to his ranches, and a new priest, Father Joseph Mut, took up his own twenty-year stay at the mission.

The poverty of the mission and its priest during this period can be seen in the re-creation of Mut's living quarters at the mission. Author James Steele, writing of a visit

to the mission in the 1880s, described the room as "gloomy, unfurnished, generally dilapidated and desolate." Today, a shabby black cloak hangs on a peg on a wall in that room as it did then. A bedraggled umbrella waits for the spring rains. Steele did note one bit of comfort, "a little bag of cheap tobacco and a wooden pipe."

Apparently, the poverty did not extend to the priest's spirit. Somehow he managed to continue the repairs. According to mission archivist Reverend William Krekelberg, Mut's ledgers show expenditures for ceiling repairs, new adobes, whitewashing, window frames, repairs to furniture and religious articles. He also rebuilt the collapsed northern wall and roof of the Serra Chapel.

Mut left the mission in 1886, going north to the mission of San Miguel Arcángel. He died three years later. Remembered more as a footnote, a poor priest living in a dingy room, he does have a gravestone of respectable size at that mission. Unfortunately, those who did him the honor misspelled his name. The man who did his best to hold his mission together for twenty years has been identified in death as Mutt.

The California missions shared his ignominy. Historical photos of Mission San Diego show it slowly falling

Father Alfred Quetu, seated on left, who entered semi-retirement in San Juan Capistrano after leaving his parish in Prescott, Arizona, presides at a celebration after a First Communion ceremony. Standing behind him is Charles Mendelson, brother of the youth who posed for *Meeting of the Cultures*, a statue alongside the Great Stone Church. The photo was taken in about 1914.

apart, brick by brick. At La Purísima almost nothing but adobe stumps would be left. At one point, San Fernando Rey de España became a hog farm. A saloon and dance hall took over the rooms of San Miguel Arcángel.

By 1890, Mission San Juan Capistrano had no resident priest. In 1891, in spite of Mut's efforts, Serra Chapel had to be abandoned, reduced to the status of a storeroom. The former *sala*, or parlor, of the Forster family became the church served by a visiting priest. Outside, the Great Stone Church stood like Roman ruins, pillar deep in rubble.

"There was nothing," remembered Richard Mendelson of the mission he knew growing up in the town of San Juan Capistrano in the early 1900s.

"Just dirt," he recalled, and, he added, "sheep."

IN THE TOWN BEYOND

In his 90s when interviewed in 2001, Richard Mendelson described his hometown as having its own goodly amount of dirt in the form of streets. He recalled the population numbering about 300 to 400 people. His family owned the place where the movie stars stayed, the Mendelson Inn. According to Mendelson, the inn had another claim to fame, the only bathtub in town.

That much has changed in San Juan Capistrano, but the feeling of a small mission town remains. As the walls came down at the mission, the walls of the town grew up, but never too high. City codes continue to regulate the height and architectural styles of the buildings near the mission. They stay at one and two stories and in styles befitting the mission period and the early years of Mexican and Anglo-American impact in the area.

In San Juan Capistrano, you can walk along *El Camino Real*, moving from the residential area north of the mission to the commercial area to the south. You can stroll the tree-lined lanes of Los Rios Historic District, west of the mission. Three of the adobe homes in the district date from the mission era. They were among the 40 built to house soldiers and mission families in the early 1790s, making San Juan Capistrano the first in the chain to allow workers to live outside the mission complex. One family never left.

Members of the Rios family have lived in the Rios Adobe since first inhabited by Feliciano Rios, who came to the mission with Serra in 1776. The Rios Adobe holds the honor as the oldest home in California continually occupied by one family.

Another adobe in the district once housed Polonia Montañez. With no resident priest at the mission in the 1890s and early 1900s, she took on the religious instruction of the town's children. She also gave them one outstanding lesson in the power of faith. In 1890, the rural town badly needed rain for the crops of hay, corn, fruit, and walnuts. When the rain didn't come, Polonia and her children went out to find it.

As the story goes, Polonia instructed the children to pray and to walk. First they made a trek to the hills to the west. The second trip took them to the canyons in the east. Finally, singing and praying, they made a trip to the beach to the south and found the answer to their prayers, tenfold. The heavens opened with such force that wagons had to be sent from the town to rescue the faithful walkers from the resulting deluge.

The town officially founded in 1841 always had a fair share of characters. One gave his name to the town. In the late 1830s and early 1840s, Santiago Argüello held the position of administrator for the mission and the town growing beyond the walls. He had a large family, many relatives and, it seems, an eye on how his bloodline could profit from his position. For a brief period of time, the people of the mission found themselves living in the pueblo of San Juan Argüello. Neither he, nor the name, stuck.

According to local stories, the early 1850s brought Joaquin Murietta to San Juan Capistrano. The robber and rustler with a Robin Hood reputation may have done some horse stealing near the town and some hiding out in the Rios Adobe. The bandit Juan Flores definitely made his appearance in 1857. The mission offered sanctuary to the townspeople while Flores and his gang looted and murdered. For his sins, he would hang.

On the right side of the law, Judge Richard Egan arrived in San Juan Capistrano in 1868 and stayed a lifetime. Born in Ireland, he joined the three other English speakers then living in the town. He worked as a surveyor for the Santa Fe Railroad, as a road commissioner, and as justice of the peace. As noted by town historian Pamela Hallan-Gibson, his surveying equipment earned its own claim to fame as having the elasticity of a "rubber chain for the rich," while the poor merited the inflexible chain of iron. The Mendelsons had their own surveying equipment to ensure, if not to question, the judge's honesty.

Judge Egan's home, the red-brick Victorian "Harmony Hall," stands on the corner of Camino Capistrano and

Forster Street and across the road from the depot for the stagecoach that ran between San Diego and Los Angeles. Local lore holds that the bricks the judge used to build the house were "left over" from the home he built for Marcos Forster, son of the man who once owned the mission.

In 1887, the Santa Fe Railroad came to town. The first major influx of tourists to San Juan Capistrano rode the trains, some carrying easels, others guidebooks. California had become a destination. James Steele sold the state in the 1887 *Rand McNally & Company's Guide to Southern California.* "It is an Eden," he told his readers.

He advised the sick and exhausted that the state offered a remedy, "better than drugs and doctors." All this could be had for $350, first class all the way from Kansas City to the delights of southern California, including San Juan Capistrano and its mission.

Today's residents remember the stories their parents and grandparents told them of the town of the early 20TH century. They remember the one about the annual Halloween prank when the youth of the town would somehow manage to get a horse-drawn carriage, minus the horse, atop the dome of the Great Stone Church. And, every Sunday morning after Halloween, the priest in the little adobe church would lean across the pulpit and announce in his own annual ritual of frustration, "AGAIN."

Residents point to the late 1950s, the freeway opening and the population boom of southern California as being a turning point for the once sleepy town where walnuts and citrus fruit had replaced acorns. Today's San Juan Capistrano has a population of 31,000, with many commuting to jobs outside the community. But, the commitment and the connection to the mission have crossed the centuries. Residents work at the mission, run businesses dependent on mission visitors, and volunteer their time for mission projects.

Even Judge Egan, with that touch of the scoundrel, made his own strong commitment to the mission. He became part of the major restoration effort that began in 1895. Two men from outside of the town of San Juan Capistrano would be instrumental in that work. The writer came first.

A part of the California Coastal Range rims San Juan Capistrano. The view looks south over the mission's entry building and down Camino Capistrano.

ARISE

On what may be a combination of First Communion and Confirmation classes, children, members of their families, friends, and clergy gather in front of the ruins of the Great Stone Church. The photograph dates to sometime between 1890 and 1900. Note that the ruins of the Great Stone Church are more intact than they are today.

CHARLES LUMMIS AND THE LANDMARKS CLUB

Los Angeles resident Charles Fletcher Lummis did almost everything. Author, editor, reporter, photographer, he wrote on Arizona's Apache Wars, the American Southwest, and Native Americans. He collected art and founded the Southwest Museum of Los Angeles. In 1895, he founded the Landmarks Club of California, dedicated "to save for our children and our children's children, the Missions and other historic monuments of California."

Lummis chose Mission San Juan Capistrano as the club's opening project, beginning work there in January 1896. By his estimates, the salvation of the mission he called "that gem of all the Missions," would cost roughly $500. The figure proved very rough, with the first $500 spent by June. Still, as he would throughout the years, Lummis made money work.

As detailed in the Rev. William Krekelberg's *San Juan Capistrano Mission Restoration, A Chronological Guide*, repairs moved forward with phenomenal speed. Four hundred fifty feet of corridors had been roofed within six months. In

that same period, major repairs were made to the old mission kitchen and the south wing of the quadrangle. Oregon pine replaced the original roof rafters of sycamore. Work on the Great Stone Church began with repairs on the columns. By July, the ever-optimistic Lummis wrote, "The ruins of the great stone church at the Mission are now saved."

The work continued into the 1900s. Repairs were made to the water system. Doors and window frames were replaced, thousands of new tiles added to the roofs. Mission walls were stabilized with turnbuckles and iron tie rods.

Lummis reported in 1902, probably without an ounce of exaggeration, that "400 tons of debris" had been removed from the Great Stone Church. In 1906, workers dealt with the sacristy, the room to the west of the altar. They repaired the cracked, small-domed ceiling with cement. Re-roofing continued to be a priority, using original tiles when possible.

Lummis gave much credit for the labor and the results to Judge Egan who worked on the roofs, built the fences

The flag and ruins rigged with scaffolds recall two tragic events – the attacks by terrorists on September 11, 2001, and an earthquake that felled the Great Stone Church in 1812, killing 40 people. As workers complete each phase of a project to stop further deterioration of the ruins, they remove the scaffolding.

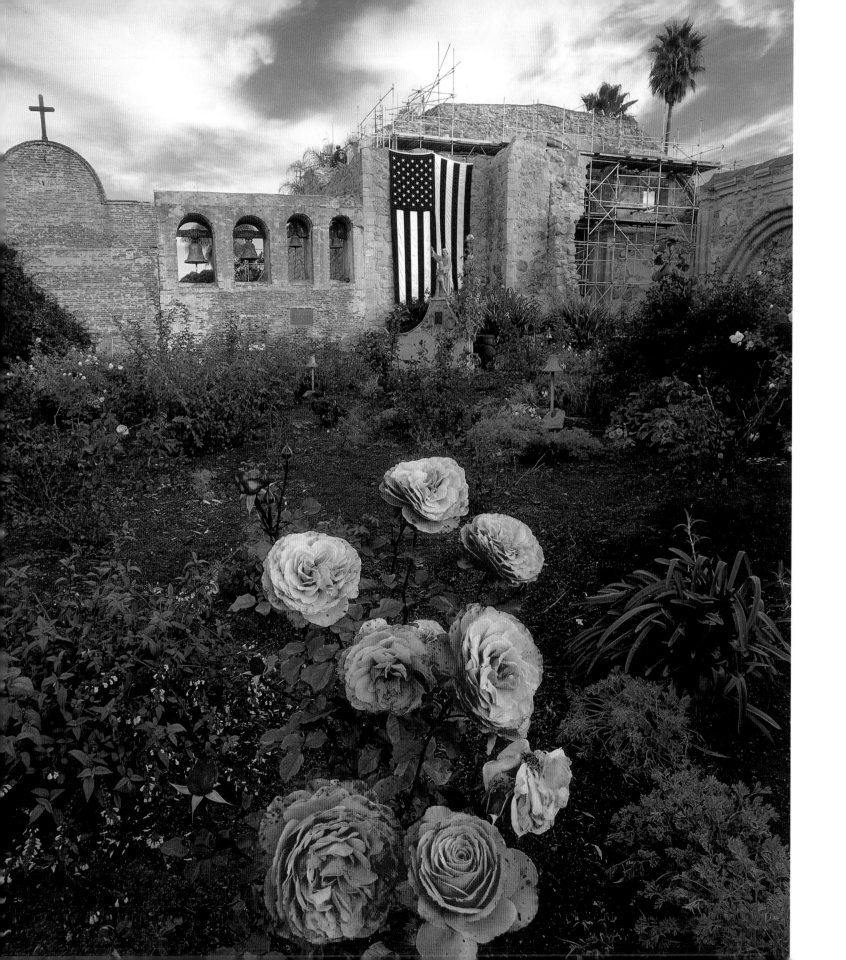

Titled *Mission San Juan Capistrano* by Elizabeth Borglum, this oil on canvas captures the elegance and strength of the mission's arches. She painted it in 1895, about two years before her husband, John Gutzon Borglum, painted *Sheep Grazing*.

Benches fashioned from stone, wood, and plaster invite visitors to sit and reflect on many of the mission's elements. Midway between the arches and the bell tower of the North Wing, lies the mission's main fountain.

and acted as a general overseer. Krekelberg does report that Egan, "used the mission property for his own agricultural purposes;" still, Lummis gave the man wings.

"Blessed, Judge Egan," he wrote of Egan whom he also noted marked each noon hour with a mint julep, "that a saint would swap his halo for.'"

Both Lummis and Egan used their contacts to do the deals and find the business owners who would supply building materials. Working at other missions as well as at San Juan Capistrano, the Landmarks Club had to depend entirely on donations.

In 1915 and again in 1916, heavy rains created havoc at the mission. An arch fell, walls collapsed. The sacristy roof at the Great Stone Church leaked, pillars crumbled. The club treasury simply didn't have the funds for repairs.

"But we are going to go ahead with it and trust to God," wrote Lummis. He firmly believed, "that a few years from now there will be men and women and boys and girls, who, without knowing us, will be glad there was someone who cared enough to save these relics of a historic past . . ."

Help usually made an appearance in the form of donations of time and talent, cartloads of gravel and lumber, and cash. In addition, the powers-that-be provided

Father St. John O'Sullivan was born in 1874 in Louisville, Kentucky. His birthday, March 19, is St. Joseph's feast day, which is the day legend says swallows annually return to the mission.

Father O'Sullivan's developments at Mission San Juan Capistrano include this fountain, the centerpiece of the Central Courtyard. Its design influenced by Moorish architecture, the Fountain of the Four Evangelists is supported by four pillars and is touched by four pathways.

invaluable assistance in a rather unprepossessing form, that of a priest suffering from tuberculosis.

RESTORATION FLOURISHES

Father St. John O'Sullivan arrived by train in 1910. He walked up the hill from the San Juan Capistrano depot, as had all of those new devotees of California tourism before him. However, he may have carried a lot less hope for the experience at the end of the hike.

O'Sullivan had tuberculosis. During a stay in a hospital in Prescott, Arizona, he met fellow patient Madeline Quetu and her visiting brother, Father Alfred Quetu, the priest for the Prescott parish.

The French-born Quetu moved to California in 1908 and purchased land in the small town of San Juan Capistrano. Semi-retired, he offered to perform the priestly duties of the nearby mission while he established a kind of colony for his relatives. But, the mission needed more help than one part-time priest, and Father Quetu suggested O'Sullivan might be the man.

"It was very still and very lonely," O'Sullivan wrote of his first night at the mission. He wasn't entirely alone. Fleas,

dogs and cats joined him as he tried to sleep in a room and then outside in a corridor. In the next few days, they would be replaced by human guests. A watercolor artist and his friend stopped at the mission that first week. Then, the men without work or a future began to arrive, the men from the road. The priest described one of them as, "the dirtiest man without exception I had ever seen."

He took them in, gave them a place to sleep and work to do. The dirt could be turned into gardens, the rooms cleaned.

By 1912, O'Sullivan could write, "I am now fairly robust." That year he published *Little Chapters About San Juan Capistrano.* The booklet cost the tourists 10 cents. A look at the mission cost them nothing. Exactly right, felt Charles Lummis, who found the idea of charging admission "very repulsive to me." But, the mission ledgers presented a strong counter-argument.

The April 1915 Mass collections from the congregation of 350 came to $35.74. Expenditures for some of the rebuilding and repairs over the next two months reached almost $400. At the end of the year, even with donations, the Bishop's subsidies, and special collections, the mission had a deficit of $530.93. Practicality had to replace sensibility. In

Workers, far left, put an addition on the south end of a barracks building, first constructed in the late 1700s to house soldiers of the Spanish empire. Artifacts, weaponry, and paintings depicting everyday life of the early era are displayed in the barracks.

1916, the mission had an admission fee, 10 cents, and a first month's gate of almost $300.

By 1917, the fee went up to s.25, and electric lights were installed. That year O'Sullivan rebuilt the south end of the barracks. By 1918 the mission had a phone, a curio shop for the tourists, and a wall closing off the front of the mission grounds. In 1919, the priest added a wall to enclose the Sacred Garden.

O'Sullivan took pleasure, as would the restorers who came after him, in using original methods and original material for repairs. He gathered up old tiles that had found their way to other buildings in the near vicinity. He did much of the work himself, and what he didn't do, he directed.

In 1922, he wrote of the results of his management: "Nine dobe-makers today are ready to lynch me."

He began rebuilding Serra Chapel, which had been abandoned for 31 years. He built a new northern wall for the church, installed the Golden Altar, and rebuilt the sanctuary. Four bodies buried near the altar were uncovered during the work, one of a parishioner and those of three priests. Father Barona, the priest who had buried the earthquake victims, had been laid to rest there, as had Father Vicente Pasqual Oliva, who died at the mission in 1848.

O'Sullivan described the fourth body as "showing signs of having been disturbed." No wonder. These were the remains of Father Fustér, carried back and forth between the two churches, buried and reburied three times during the less-than-quiet opening years of his eternal rest.

Father St. John O'Sullivan died in 1933 at age 59, due to complications from his old ailment. He had restored Serra Chapel, built a mission school, created gardens, and installed fountains that still splash today. The little booklet he wrote in 1912 sold 40,000 copies in 15 years. The artists he invited in carried the vision of the mission out to the world. Like Lummis and Egan before him, O'Sullivan raised money and found willing contributors of materials and locals who would lend him their wagons and equipment for use at the mission. And, he utilized the media.

In one radio address, he told the story of his first birthday at the mission. A little lonesome perhaps, he claimed to have been cheered by the guests who did arrive, the swallows. The date would have been March 19, 1911, his birthday, St. Joseph's day, the day another priest once waited for the sails of a ship to touch the horizon. The swallows had equal right to celebrate the date. They had returned.

FLIGHTS OF FANCY

PETER ENSENBERGER

THE SWALLOWS
OF SAN JUAN CAPISTRANO

Acu, the last full-blooded Juaneño, told Father O'Sullivan about the swallows of San Juan Capistrano. He told him they came every year on the feast day of Saint Joseph. He told the priest they flew from Jerusalem, carrying a twig on which they could rest on the ocean. O'Sullivan told the story to writer Charles Saunders who published it in the 1930 book *Capistrano Nights, Tales of a California Mission Town.*

O'Sullivan added to the story. He told Saunders that he had seen someone in the town knocking down the nests of the swallows, calling them "dirty birds." As he had done with the artists, the priest extended an invitation.

" 'Then come on, swallows, come to the mission,' I cried, 'I'll give you shelter. Come to the mission, there's room enough for all.' "

The truth amid the tales proves no less beguiling. The cliff swallows, *petrochelidon pyrrhonota,* make their yearly pilgrimage to the valley of San Juan Capistrano from the marshy agricultural land of northeast Argentina, Uruguay, and Brazil. They fly up to 3,000 miles with no twigs upon which to rest. They do arrive, always, around March 19 and stay until fall.

The 5- to 7-inch birds with blue-gray heads and wings, white bellies and square tails, make gourd-like nests of mud and saliva. The females lay four to five eggs, with the males assisting in the care of the young. The land around San Juan Capistrano has long supplied all the prerequisites for the swallows' summer stay, dirt and water for the mud nests and insects on which to dine. The swallows also need suitable surfaces for their nests. For many years, the mission met the need with its overhanging tile roofs and the crags and corners of the Great Stone Church.

Those who practice the gentle sport of birding have studied the swallows in this valley since the early 1900s, but *Capistrano Nights* drew the attention of a larger audience. The *Los Angeles Times* picked up the story. Then, in 1937, NBC Radio broadcast live from the mission on the day of the birds' promised return. Songwriter Leon Rene heard the radio report about waiting for the swallows to come back to Capistrano as he waited for breakfast in his Los

Festivals throughout the year draw tens of thousands of visitors to Mission San Juan Capistrano. Mariachis, above, and audience, right, are gathered for a "return of the swallows" celebration. Other annual festivals include the Lincoln celebration (recalling the signing of documents by President Lincoln to deed the mission back to the church); the Russian heritage celebration (recalling that Russian ambitions prompted the Spaniards to settle California and thus establish Mission San Juan Capistrano); and a flower and garden show (starring the gardening work of volunteers). Details about events are available on the mission's Web site (www.missionsjc.com) or by calling (949) 234-1300.

PETER ENSENBERGER

In recent years, the mission's famed swallows have returned in sparse numbers for the March celebration, but the crowds wait and celebrate nonetheless.

Angeles home. According to his son Rafael, Rene decided, "That would be a great title for a song."

Everything about the 1939 *When the Swallows Come Back to Capistrano* worked. A soft tune with an air of country and western and a touch of Mexico, the song caught the ear of the public and the voices of a host of artists. Glenn Miller made a recording, so did the Ink Spots, Pat Boone, the King Sisters, Xavier Cougat, Gene Autry and yes, Elvis Presley.

Visitors to the mission today might not remember the words, probably not even the first few notes, almost definitely not the name of the writer, but some do remember the subject and the title of the song. They look for the swallows.

Tens of thousands of people travel to the mission during the third weekend in March for the celebration of the swallows' return. They fill the patios, watch dancers and look at the work of local artists. However, in past years almost all of the guests of honor have gone elsewhere.

The older residents of San Juan Capistrano remember large flocks of hundreds of birds. Even younger members of the community remember a time when swallows dove through the arches of the mission. But, by the end of

the 20TH century, the swallows of the mission seemed to be reduced to a quick passing flicker in the sky above the buildings.

Work done in the early 1990s to make mission buildings better able to resist earthquake damage resulted in the destruction of the nests the swallows returned to year after year. They still came back to the valley, hundreds nesting on the buildings of a nearby community college as well as on homes and businesses, but only a handful returned to the mission. In order to tempt them back, the mission administration undertook a swallow restoration project in 2001, complete with the experts and the technology.

Facsimile nests went up as did tape-recorded calls of the swallows during the travel season, a kind of "This is the place, folks" advertisement for any fellow birds flying over the mission. The gardening priority list at the mission also added keeping the necessities of the swallow life easily accessible.

Cliff swallow expert Dr. Charles Brown of the University of Tulsa advised the mission on swallow restoration. He did not feel that the thousands of human visitors would make a difference in the swallows' decision to return. When it comes to people, he said, "These are reasonably tolerant

The mission's attempt to lure more swallows has had some success. Perhaps the birds are becoming aware that they are the stars of a major mission event.

birds." However, the process of enticing the swallows back will take patience and time.

Other birds — sparrows, hummingbirds, doves, crows, black phoebes, house finches and pigeons — have stayed at the mission. One among them managed to make his mark in mission history. Call him "Kru-ku," and say the name the way he might, high pitched with a strong roll to the letter *r*, like the love song of a pigeon.

KRU-KU

He fell in love at Mission San Juan Capistrano in the year 2000. He chose someone way out of his league, Klara Macciotta, an art conservator working on the Great Stone Church. He didn't care. This common variety gray pigeon attached himself to his lady fair, literally locking himself onto her shoulder. He would not be dislodged. Karla left the mission that night with Kru-ku hanging on while she assured the women who watch the front gate, "I'm not stealing this bird." But she had stolen his heart.

She returned with the bird the a few days later, and then made her getaway, driving the five miles to her home.

It took him more than a day, but with homing in his blood as well as loving, Kru-ku found the house. Klara accepted the inevitable, saying, "Okay, we want to be together."

So, they would be from that time forward, at work, at home, together. Look up. Kru-ku may be watching his lady from a perch on the arches or near the dome of the Great Stone Church. He may be willing to alight and allow another human to touch him, to pat his head. Or, he may be gone. A wild pigeon lives a few good years, if he's lucky. In love, a pigeon can live forever, as a story born within the walls of the mission.

SPIRITS

The people of the mission and the mission town tell the stories of the humans who never left, not even in death. A supervisor working on the Great Stone Church once felt a tug as he climbed a ladder within the dome. He kept going, got another tug and got the message. He went back down. He, like others, had also heard heavy footsteps behind him when walking on the paths of the mission.

Michael Gastelum, the keeper of the bells, speaks of

The lore of Mission San Juan Capistrano includes accounts of humans being approached by spirits. A mission craftsman working atop the Great Stone Church, right, once felt tugs as he climbed a ladder. He and others also have heard heavy footsteps behind them as they walked the mission's paths.

Viewed from the Great Stone Church, opposite page, a crowd enjoys a celebration in the Central Courtyard, a focal point of the community of San Juan Capistrano. The town has prohibited buildings from the upper level of the hills forming the niche in which the town and mission reside. The intent is to preserve the view from mission grounds.

his father's experience at the mission, "He'd seen the headless one," and of his own experiences within Serra Chapel. "You'd walk through and you could hear the pews . . . like someone was getting out of them."

Before she died, Buena Ventura Albertina Garcia Nieblas prophesied her return to Mission San Juan Capistrano. She told her grandson Jerry Nieblas, "If you are ever on the grounds and feel a pat on your back, it's going to be me."

She explained the roaming spirits of the mission as, "people who hadn't finished a problem." Some haven't finished their work. Folklore has a Spanish soldier still patrolling the grounds, a man with heavy booted steps.

Even the Sacred Garden, that place of serenity, comes with a ghost story. Two young people had fallen in love and saw each other against their parents' wishes. The girl did penance by carrying a candle in front of the congregation going to early Mass on December 8, 1812. In the story, she died in the earthquake, but her spirit can sometimes be seen looking out of the church window over the Sacred Garden. She still carries her candle.

Another girl wanders in legends of the town. Denise Duprez, niece of Father Quetu, died in a fire in 1914. They

say her spirit walks on the hilltop near her burial site. Others speak of the chanting woman and the weeping woman and the young boy who watches the workers at the Great Stone Church.

The people of the mission tell these stories in a matter-of-fact style, perhaps with a small laugh or smile, but without fear. The spirits do not seem to be malevolent. After all, according to Buena Ventura Albertina Garcia Nieblas, some were "people who were so much in love with this place that they would never leave it."

As for the tap she predicted her grandson might one day feel as he walked through the mission his family never left?

"Twice," he says with a nod. "Twice."

. . . AND OTHER TALES

For a few years, the bandit Joaquín Murieta became part of mission folklore. His name had been found carved high on an outer wall of the Great Stone Church with the date 1865. Some believed the bandit could have clamored up the wall, hanging from a rope to leave his chiseled calling card. If this proved true, a new chapter

84

or at least a paragraph could be added to California history. According to historical accounts, Murieta died in 1853, killed by California rangers. They brought in his head and the hand of his bandit companion, Three-Fingered Jack.

Not good enough, some said back then. That wasn't his head, and the man Murieta traveled with should rightly have been called Four-Fingered Jack, having lost only one digit. So, perhaps he didn't die and did climb up the stone face of the church years later.

The potential legend died in 2001 with a local resident admitting responsibility. He, not the bandit, had carved the name 35 years before. Still, others would say the bandit could have left something behind. He could have left treasure.

Treasure tales have long attached themselves to the old missions of the Spanish empire. Sometimes they involve the belief that the priests had mines in the hills, be those hills in California, Arizona, or Mexico.

If not the gold of the padres, the tales turn to bandits and their treasure troves. At Mission San Juan Capistrano they had the pirate Bouchard and the legend that after his men wobbled back to the ship, he left his ill-gotten goods behind somewhere near the beach. Why he would do that

and then sail back to a life in Argentina remains unexplained.

In the past, people dug for treasure within the mission grounds. They may have seen the lights, the ones said to dance, flicker, and rise over the spot where treasure could be found. That type of mission groundbreaking ended in the late 20TH century with new walls and security, but something had been left behind more than a century ago, something to be prized.

A horseshoe sits atop the dome of the Great Stone Church, probably put in the cement during the Landmarks Club's restoration in the late 1890s and early 1900s. Workers may have used the horseshoe to mark a crack in the dome. Or, they may have had other reasons, the kind that come when you work without a net.

A new generation of workers covered the dome with a lead cap in 2001 as a protection against the elements, but they didn't touch the horseshoe. They left it there, safe in cement, guarded by lead.

In a place of spirits and dancing lights and footsteps down corridors, of bandits and pirates and birds who fly thousands miles and others who fall madly in love, one doesn't easily toss away a piece of luck.

THE NEXT GENERATION

BOTH BY PETER ENSENBERGER

T he men and women who hold the mission steady against the onslaught of time and nature talk a lot about what might have been. At the Great Stone Church two men in hard hats, T-shirts and blue jeans ponder where a wall might have stood a hundred years ago. They have no document, no sketch to provide an answer.

In the room under the bell tower of the new church, an archivist, a historian, and an archaeologist ponder how much of the floor of the Great Stone Church may have been covered with diamond-shaped tiles. Surrounded by books, they still must speculate.

"In my lifetime, in my career, I will never have a project that is any more difficult than this one," states preservation architect John Loomis of his work on the Great Stone Church. He has been involved with the mission since 1989, when the latest major restoration and stabilization project began.

Each step taken to stabilize and preserve this mission ends up creating a stairway. A formula for the mud "skin" used on the outside of the barracks required a year of trial and error. The repair of a single wall at the Great Stone Church took five design concepts.

Once the largest stone structure west of the Mississippi River, now a ravaged relic . . . the Great Stone Church at Mission San Juan Capistrano has flourished in the light, and it has endured the shadows. Built by people of the mission under the direction of two priests, it was completed in nine years, in 1806. An earthquake brought most of it down six years later, killing 40 worshipers during morning Mass.

Now the remains are held together by reinforcing devices, above, so that future generations can appreciate its magnificently arched construction, top.

Mornings at the mission are an especially calm, meditative time. The graceful scene, left, belies the decay in places away from easy view, such as the Great Stone Church's sanctuary, right.

As powerful as it may have once appeared, the Great Stone Church now requires a delicate touch. With no protecting roof, the walls have crumbled. The mortar has turned to dust. The rubble fill between the double walls has settled, leaving deep cavities between them. Because of the fragile condition of the ruins, pneumatic drills cannot be used. Workers use slower rotary drills. Conservators use dental picks to find the cracks and voids, and they inject grout into the walls with syringes to preserve the structure, to keep it standing, to save a piece of history.

Archaeologist Harry Francisco holds to three rules for work at the mission:

Do No Damage;
The Work Should Be Reversible;
Don't Fool the Public.

Under the first rule, materials should be compatible to the structure and existing materials. Workers use original materials whenever possible on the Great Stone Church. They mix lime-based mortar with original mortar. They use the original stones, often moved in the old way, with the strength of their backs.

The men and women working on the scaffolding of the Great Stone Church also keep their eye on the future.

PETER ENSENBERGER

Conservators who come after them will be able to reverse the work being done now. For example, stainless steel rods are used to stabilize the walls of the church. Carbon fiber would offer five times the tensile strength, but the fittings needed to attach the carbon fiber to the intrastructure have not been invented. So, the stainless steel rods have been placed in sleeves. When technology catches up with the innovation of the workers on this project, the rods can be pulled out and replaced with the best the future has to offer.

And, following the third rule, they don't pass off new work as being original to the structure. Colors and textures of materials used in repairs may be closely matched but not to the point of obliterating the reality of the ruins. Carvings are not exact replications. This commitment to allowing the scars of time to remain can be seen throughout the mission. Pillars, arches, and walls have not been made shopping-mall pristine with a brand-new coat of mortar. You can see the bones of this mission.

"We're not trying to decorate history," states mission administrator Gerald Miller. Still, just holding a mission in time can cost a great deal of money. As Miller describes the situation, "We have 225 years of deferred maintenance here."

In 1886, Charles Lummis estimated no less than $100,000 would be needed to restore the Great Stone Church, a jaw-dropping sum in those days. Twenty-first-century reality proves equally stunning. A recent restoration of 30 feet of wall at the ruins cost $1.8 million. To hold together what remains of the structure will take more than $7 million. Millions had to be spent on the 1990s seismic retrofit of the mission to make the buildings more resistant to earthquakes. Roofs had to be rebuilt to make them part of the structures. Walls had to be strengthened with steel beams. Steel cables locked into cement anchors now run over the roof of Serra Chapel to stabilize the church in case of earthquake. While the old church may never float away, it still has a decided tilt to the left.

The millions of dollars necessary for continued mission restoration and preservation comes from private and public donations and state and federal government sources. Some donations still arrive in the forms Charles Lummis and Father St. John O'Sullivan knew so well, gifts of supplies and gifts of time. More than 100 residents of the town and surrounding communities serve as mission docents. They lead the tours, often for the children of California.

The fourth-grade curriculum of California public schools includes an extensive study of the history, the native

ALL BY PETER ENSENBERGER

people, and the geography of the state. With so much history and cultural impact tied to the Spanish missions, school children often take mission field trips. At Mission San Juan Capistrano, the docents keep their own eyes on the future. They meet the children at the gate.

One type of gift to the mission falls outside the norm of cash, building materials, and volunteerism. The true treasures of the mission, the religious and historic articles, disappeared over the years. They ended up in private hands, often of those who wanted to keep them safe from looters. Some have made their way back to the mission. Many of the religious articles used on the altar were returned in the 1990s, including two altar candlesticks that came back to the mission in a bag. The donor didn't leave a name. Sometimes mission property or materials related to mission history can be purchased. Other times, those who search for these remnants of the past can only wait and hope.

In the room under the bell tower of the basilica, a story is told of an archivist visiting the home of a prominent citizen who happened to own a document of mission history. When the archivist arrived, a voice called out from the interior of the house, "You're not going to get it." And, he didn't. Not yet.

They shake their heads, these people of the mission. The archaeologist sits in his dusty office surrounded by documents and broken pieces of history. "There's just so much we don't know," he muses.

On the scaffolding, the mason stares at the wall before him speculating on why the stones were placed in a certain way. "You have to wonder," he says softly.

They don't know what happened to the original bells of the mission, the ones buried at the first founding. They don't know exactly where that founding or the second one took place. They don't know what the Great Stone Church looked like when finished, nor what happened to the first altar of the little adobe church. What they do know beyond any question has to do with the sense of this mission, the soul, and how it touches them.

"I ask for the mission to take care of me," says Bernie Bobitch, mason and supervisor at the Great Stone Church. He says he sings each morning as he goes to work, the way the Juaneño, the soldiers, and the priests sang on their mornings two hundred years ago.

THE NEXT GENERATION 91

EPILOGUE

"We're going to walk through this mission," the docent tells his young charges. "We're going to see how people lived in the 1700s and 1800s."

"Very peaceful," a woman comments as she looks across the Entry Courtyard. "The tools they had to work with and what they created . . ." The words drift off with her gaze.

"They've got a long way to go," says the tourist staring up at the Great Stone Church.

"They are just trying to preserve what's left," a docent explains.

"Isn't this something," another tourist comments as he walks down the path of stones where the names have been carved in love and memory.

A woman dressed in native costume laughs and sings and tells the visitors stories of her people, the Acjachemen. Mission bells ring out the hours, and mission workers turn to their song.

"It's still like it used to be," says a schoolgirl standing at the fountain in the Central Courtyard. "No one changed it."

"Okay, everyone, we're going to go this way now," the docent calls, and a parade of children forms. They march briskly down the path radiating from the fountain and move into the shadows of the long arcade. Behind them the voices of the mission rise ever upward like the songs of the birds and the glow of the candles in a little mission church.

The artistry at Mission San Juan Capistrano blends the shapes, textures, and designs of structures with well groomed flora. Designs such as this one on a bench in front of the North Wing are seen throughout the mission.

INDEX